Psychotherapy
from the Center:

A Humanistic View
of Change and of Growth

Psychotherapy
from the Center:

A Humanistic View
of Change and of Growth

RAHE B. CORLIS
Department of Psychiatry
The Ohio State University

PETER RABE
California State Polytechnic College
San Luis Obispo

INTERNATIONAL TEXTBOOK COMPANY
Scranton, Pennsylvania

Standard Book Number 7002 2204   9

We dedicate this book
to
LINDA, BARBARA, and ?

Foreword

The old doc waving his magic wand and the researcher with his data charts are spawning a new generation of psychotherapists. The clinician who could evaluate his hunch and use his intuitive processes is succeeded by a professional who can "care" with all his being. This is a new generation. As in aerodynamics, a generation in the evolution of psychotherapy is over in ten years. The teacher is out-dated and his students have moved on to new patterns and new styles of being.

First the observers gave way to the data collectors. The baton was passed on to the microscopists and the theoreticians. Now specialists in the applied art and the applied science of psychotherapy are rapidly coining a methodology for the process of treatment—derived from psychiatry and psychology, yet not symbiotic with either.

The philosophical anlage of existentialism has made a giant step in organizing the percepts and experiential thrust with which this new generation is coining a new therapy. The authors provide us with the next thrust. To read such phenomenology and existentialism is a bit like wading into the new mathematics. It's obviously pertinent and yet it feels so strange that the daily life of practice won't jibe with it. I can't put my feet in those shoes even with a shoehorn.

The new language sounds foreign and creaky. The system seems to do violence to our secret conclusions of last year. The authors talk from the teacher's podium. The format is systematic, the style patterned yet not painful. These men are craftsmen in the essay writing so standard in psychiatry and psychology. They present in a simple manner a cogent tale of practical, even homey experience and evaluation. The linkage in thought quietly moves to a critical level and the reader is suddenly plunged into the process of discovery and enlightenment. Few people dare to talk about the here and now in the language of today at noon. A sense of drama is imparted by the offer of data from the therapist's own living with himself and with his patients.

Those double binds, like "impersonal empathy" and "confrontation must continue throughout treatment" act like a good aperitif. They whet the appetite.

Psychiatry and psychology have moved from the world of research to the world of treatment. The move is to an activated therapist pattern. We were trying to find out about people, then about combinations of people, whether in marriages or families or groups or communities. Now we are trying to change those units from what they are to what they want to be, to untie them where they were and allow them the freedom to move. The book is fun reading because the authors put themselves on the line. There are reams of talk about the process of psychotherapy, yet these authors move in the world of phenomenology, of existential thought, of Zen orientation, and do it in the framework of direct statements, rules of thumb, and such comfortable words as trust and contact. There's a touching physical sense in their word "contact;" the periphery of my skin and your skin. They speak of these in the contrasting framework of the center of my being and the center of your being. They use these words "center" and "periphery" as roughly similar to the words "fantasy" and "reality" and yet "contact" is so much better and more interpersonal! Contact and the degree of contact makes discussion of withdrawal so much more simple. They talk with a full awareness of the usefulness of the therapist as prototype.

The book is not easy reading, although the beauty of the language makes it a joy to read. It is not a do-it-yourself kit for the young psychotherapist as "Client-centered Therapy" was taken to be.

The authors talk directly to the experienced therapist. For those who have begun to see through their own simplistic techniques and the glossy print success of their early years this is very valuable. The thoughtful clinician who is ready to reevaluate his own work will find this book a tremendous asset. The writing is nicely divided between theory and technique. It is often innovative and catalytic. The descriptive bits include detail and suggestive case fragments, for the young and for the uncommitted therapist. The theory is uniquely poetic and the case fragments make concrete the theoretical points which are both broad and deep; and therefore, are hard to grasp. At times the writing seems very exciting. Best of all they don't talk *about* therapy, they talk therapy. They talk of the here and now in the present tense. This highlights for me the significance of a first book about existential therapy in the down-to-earth experience of day-to-day practice, rather than in the exotic words of the philosopher.

The continuum of defense and creativity leads to a contrast of the "ought" world and the "being" world, with a freshness of word use unique in our scientific land of old cliches and trite rules. The authors are adroit debunkers. Many bright points of insight and technique are contributed while the derivations from Martin Buber, Carl Rogers, and Professor Husserl shine through.

The authors move from considerations of the patient to techniques of the process to the person of the therapist with an ease that imparts a sense of the unity of all three. The use of spoken language also aids in breaking through into the existential world. Although they don't integrate their therapeutic concepts with the analytic mode, this does no violence to modern psychotherapeutic thought. The integration of therapy with pathology is ragged and fragmentary in places but this is a trademark of the professional therapist as contrasted with the research-oriented analyst. The tangential excursion into pathology is refreshing and many times creative. Respect for the patient as a person is clear and solid.

The sense of deja vu that I as a therapist get in moving from line to line and paragraph to paragraph is a most exciting one. It's as though an old married couple are describing the growth of their love-life and you feel in your own bones the changes and the process that you've gone through by being touched, stroked, and titillated. Dr. Corlis and Dr. Rabe use a kind of present tense in their writing which makes it neither an essay nor a ponderous Germanic theory, nor yet a simple fairy tale. Most important, it is not an existential treatise, or a psychoanalytic dissection, it's just good down-to-earth talk from therapist to therapist and it opens up windows and sunlit areas which were previously dark blue or at least hazy and foggy.

CARL A. WHITAKER, M.D.

Professor of Psychiatry
University of Wisconsin
Madison, Wisconsin

A Note to the Reader

Most of this book is not for the casual reader. It is for the reader who is psychotherapeutically oriented, who wants to participate in psychological change and in personal growth—which is about as serious as one can get.

We wish to describe a psychotherapeutic orientation and a technique. We do not make theories and will not argue with theories. We do neither because our concern is with experiential events and with ways of knowing them. We distinguish such an event from its theoretical distillate or from its classification name, neither of which is the substance of the psychotherapeutic encounter itself. If we can sharpen the distinction between an event and a concept about it, then we have contributed something of worth.

At times it may seem as if we were giving short shrift to other writers in the field, including the innovators, the brilliant ones. The patent fact that we have learned from them often gives best evidence of our regard for them.

Our lack of references to historical antecedents has a purpose. Our infrequent use of cross-matching the views or conclusions of others has been done with intent. We want to introduce the existential approach of our method—existentially. In the concrete, that means that we want to present the psychotherapeutic encounter as it occurs and as it is experienced. This purpose is not served by meeting a novel event in the context of what is already known. Instead, we will describe an approach into the novel situation of each encounter without the contamination of viewing the event in terms of its sameness to something else. The manner in which this book is written has this immediacy of experience as its aim. How to confront the uniqueness of the psychotherapeutic event is the topic of this book. We regard the event of psychotherapeutic encounter less as an instance of proper technique and more as a creative moment which meets its own needs. For that reason we will have to stress the state of the therapist more than his professional bag of tricks or his memory for proper techniques.

It should go without saying that our omissions of references which by custom and courtesy are usually included in books of this sort are not meant as slights. For that matter, the work of others is much better in the original than in any digest by us. We do believe, of course, that we have something important to say. That may sound like arrogance, but it is also the only reason why anyone should write a book.

RAHE B. CORLIS
PETER RABE

Columbus, Ohio
December, 1968

Contents

Psychotherapy
from the Center:
**A Humanistic View
of Change and of Growth**

chapter 1

Perspective and Purpose

THE SPIRIT OF PHENOMENOLOGY AND OF EXISTENTIALISM

Man's emphatic need to orient himself has long found expression in the regimes of philosophy. In the mood of our time the personal crisis of disorientation has become the job of psychotherapy.

Traditionally, the philosopher's tendency to use abstractions to conceptualize *about* the experience of man has too often remained essentially meaningless to the man who is critically losing his good sense of self. A contrasting direction of inquiry has been developed by E. G. Husserl (1859-1938). He formally states in his *Phenomenology* (1913; English trans. 1931) that a concept *about* experience will mirror the experience itself only in part. Husserl developed a method of inquiry in which the experience is not distorted through conceptualization. In essence, his method insists that you *stay with* the experience itself, allowing it to unfold and to reveal itself.

Experience must be understood from the inside. Subjectivity is the raw material of our inspection. If this subjective experience of what is known to us here-and-now remains absent or vague, then the methods of objectivity have truly nothing to scrutinize. A meaningful philosophy of man must in this sense be grounded in the individual's immediate, living experience. This is the meaning of the phenomenological emphasis on "the here-and-now."

We make this same emphasis in our approach to psychotherapy.

Here-and-now means the experience of our focus at this very moment. The experience includes the knowledge that this moment is in continual change. Therefore the phenomenological emphasis in our psychotherapeutic work is placed on the ongoing, immediate experience of both patient and therapist as they interact.

This concern with man as he is in his world, this nonjudging experience of a subject event, is the existential experience. The total phenomena experienced at any moment in time describes man's existential situation.

Our work in psychotherapy looks for this experienced event. This approach is phenomenological because we want to know the event before it is altered with explanations.

A WARNING ON THE USE OF THEORY
IN PSYCHOTHERAPY

It is the chief function of a theory to sharpen the focus on the object of inquiry.

Psychotherapeutic inquiry tends to rest heavily upon a theory of personality—such as Freud's—and upon its derived clinical method, such as psychoanalysis. The focusing device in a theoretical system is that theory's set of criteria which measure the relative importance of what is being observed. Therefore a theory will tend to ignore what is theoretically unimportant. For example, psychoanalysis lays no great stress on the unique qualities of social interaction. Therefore the orthodox analyst avoided its consequences by keeping out of the patient's view. In contrast, Harry Stack Sullivan emphasizes the therapist's role as a "participant observer" in the psychotherapeutic session. The stress on social interaction in his theory takes the practical form of interacting vis-à-vis the patient.

The primary event in the psychotherapeutic situation is the encounter between patient and therapist. This encounter between two human beings does not exist, nor is its importance known, before it is allowed to occur. And its occurrence will be instantly altered, if not limited, by the introduction of a prearranged focus which in this case is supplied by a personality theory.

But there is a time and a use for the selective function of theories—*after* the psychotherapeutic encounter has been allowed to occur with a minimum of judgment. The phenomenological therapist is first of all concerned with the patient's existential situation. He must allow himself to receive what he might not expect, what he might not understand. He must allow the patient to unfold what no theory can predict with individual accuracy: the unique self.

Only then, when this contact without ideals for guidance and without judgments for safety has come to exist, can the tools of theory be gently applied to the stuff that has been given. Unfortunately, not any one theory will do.

REDUCTIONISM AND HOLISM

We will take one simplifying view of the many orientations in psychotherapy. It is only a first view, but for the purposes of this book it can be our last.

It is enough to orient ourselves by viewing two major directions which are basic to personality theories in psychotherapy today: the reductionistic approach, and the holistic approach.

The reductionistic attitude is well represented by the psychoanalytical tradition whose insights gave impetus to the major personality theories of today and whose analytical explanations have led to workable methods of treatment.

The psychoanalytical approach is at all times intent on finding the most important, single factor in the workings of the human being, which, in the psychoanalytic view, is regarded as a closed system. This intent makes the approach reductionistic. All ramifications of the psychological being derived ultimately from one basic variable, the sexual instinct and its fate. Every pertinent argument on the topic is a variation on this reductionistic theme.

The reductionistic approach has one defect which we ourselves would like to avoid. It is the dissection of an experience, the act which destroys the meaning of the experience as a whole.

The gestalt of an experience is different from the elements that are a product of its analysis. A religious experience, for example, may have personal meanings other than the sexual and aggressive content derived by psychoanalytical scrutiny. The pertinent meaning may be entirely ideographic. Such a meaning is by necessity missed by a reductionistic analysis which looks for the least common denominator. Since the idiographic, unclassified meaning of an experience may well disappear—explained away, as it were by reduction—the reductionistic analysis may overlook major, motivating factors in a given personality.

A reductionistic analysis finds its justification in determinism. For example, it is one of the fundamental tenets of psychoanalysis that all psychic phenomena are the necessary results of previously existing conditions. Consequently a deterministic position obviates the existence, let alone the relevance, of free will.

Free will, in our usage, is the instance in the ongoing experience when choice is possible or when an impetus for choice exists. Within the limits of our realistic capacities this instance of choice can give direction to the individual's growth, or nongrowth. A reductionist theory, embedded as it is within its deterministic context, has no room for the potential of man's self-directed growth, or for any significant sense of personal responsibility.

It is true that many behaviors are conditioned, but many need not be.

Psychoanalytic reductionism must view subjective experience—such as sense of freedom, meaningfulness, hope—as epiphenomena or illusions which have no significance in themselves. They are illusions which are therapeutically treated as such. The focus of attention in an existential approach to psychotherapy treats the so-called epiphenomenon as a quality of the here-and-now experience, rather than a quantity derived from a history of cause and effect.

For another example, note that any deterministic approach dictates that a symbol be reduced to its constituent parts (again, to cause-and-effect relationships primarily), while phenomenological therapy works with a symbol on the level on which it occurs. To reduce a symbol means to alter the existential meaning which it has for its creator. Rather than attaining an interpretive gain, the reduction may constitute a loss in meaning. There is an obvious analogy: the properties of hydrogen and those of oxygen are not the qualities of H_2O. The qualities of their combined form—a form that exists in its own right, so to speak—are significantly different from either "constituent" when in isolation.

Analysis per se is not the high road to understanding. Any analytical approach is posited on a directed question which prescribes the limits of its answer. A question such as, "What is the mood of this dance, how does it feel to move in such ways?" receives scant answer via an analysis of the musculature used in the execution of the dance. In other words, there are relevant meanings which either do not exist, or which are lost, on the road of reduction.

The orientation which can avoid the reductionist error is *holism*. Our work falls within its scope. In our usage, holism is the assertion that the organism has characteristics germane to itself alone. Instead of describing a house by its bricks, a neurosis by its infantile tributaries, such factors are viewed in the context of the now-existing unity which we encounter.

Carl Rogers and Abraham Maslow are two psychologists who have made major contributions to a holistic orientation. They speak of the psychological organism as a functional whole which is doing something in a present situation. Their limited reliance upon deterministic aids and their emphasis upon man as an existential entity have generated therapeutic techniques that emphasize, and stimulate choice much more than psychoanalytical techniques are apt to do.

The nonreductionistic approach exemplifies the sort of exploration of the here-and-now which leads to an awareness of *what is*. For example, since any subjective experience is an acceptable datum in phenomenology, a religious experience can be handled on the level on which it occurs without necessary postulations about the existence of God. The inquiry loses its topheavy load of theological speculation but expands an awareness of the individual's religious state.

The phenomenological approach is not issue-centered. It is subject-centered.

TWO ORGANISMIC STATES

To view the organism as a whole is not a recommendation for treating it as something like primordial slime. We recognize what is there, namely differential functioning aspects of the whole. These aspects (called *parts* by others) may work harmoniously, by which we mean that the integrity of the whole is preserved. This organism hangs together. It is psychologically healthy. It grows, it changes continuously as it participates in the process we call life. When the individual stops functioning as an integrated whole which flows with the ever-changing processes of life, then we describe a personality which becomes rigid, immutable, whose aspects split out of the whole and assume a pseudolife of their own.

But it must be remembered that any personality, no matter how inefficient its self-maintenance, no matter how unsuccessful its functions, is nevertheless in a state of organization. There are discernible principles of organization in the workings of the most unhappy and the most disturbed individual. In fact, the very immutability of their organization—the quality that leads to a high degree of predictability in behavior—may be a criterion of just how remote they are from a viable capacity to move with the changing demands of their lives. The self-preservation of the organism under reduced viability is served by a significant if not intentional reduction in the effective demands placed on the organism. Disbalancing impulses are curtailed through control. The impact of the environment is reduced via insensitivities. An increasingly shrunken life-space and life-function is the price we pay for maintaining by hook or by crook some manner of internal balance while under stress. The very exaggeration of pathological states is evidence of the lengths to which the organism can go in an effort to maintain itself.

We have described an extreme of self-maintenance, where the payment for some manner of balance at any cost results in the sort of condition which we find in a patient. The effort at self-preservation need not be that critical (which is precisely the hope which brings the patient into therapy). There is, in brief, the condition of doing something about one's situation; then there is a state where organization has been achieved, where all battles seem to have been won, when no future battles can demand more than an available strength. To speak schematically for the moment, we would now like to describe these two organismic states, the one of achieving, and the one of having achieved. We will call them, respectively, the state of *operating at the periphery* and the state of *being at center*. The viable pendulum swing of organic life moves from one to the other.

THE FUNCTIONS AND FATES AT THE PERIPHERY

The periphery of the psychological being is the area where contact occurs. It is the personality aspect of reactive moods, of planning and thinking which concerns daily needs; it is the area of encounter by habit. The need for survival action and action for survival occurs at the periphery. At the periphery resides the intent and the implementation of doing something about the world. It is there that self-preservation is implemented, either by reaching for something or by warding off something. All calculations, appraisals, and judgments reside there. All scheming, manipulating, influencing, and forcing alterations into being take place on the periphery. All moods which underlie action and all habits which reduce the effort of continued attending constitute the periphery.

The more you live on the periphery the more you alter the world as it is. These descriptions, aside from stating that this aspect of the personality functions in the name of self-preservation, suggest also the potential pathology.

In the planning for action we must enter fantasy, and in the switch to fantasy we enter the as-if level of our world. This world has the advantage of being an uncommitted state of action. It is only preparatory to an encounter with the world, which is of course one of the beauties of planning. But then, this as-if world has its own rewards. If the threat of committed action seems large enough, then the as-if satisfactions of fantasy can become a much more attractive second best. They may satisfy to the exclusion of action. However, on the evidence of long wards filled with psychotics, the method pays off with rapidly diminishing returns.

There are less stringent and more frequent examples of the individual who acts on the basis of a fiction. He acts as if the world owes him a living; he comes on like the greatest asset to man and/or women; he acts out the role of being the scum of the earth; he convinces everyone and himself that he is the most hateful or hated. We all have a repertoire of fictions about ourselves which vary with our fluctuating ability to stay in touch with ourselves and the world.

Our cultural emphasis on the periphery is well-nigh exclusive, heavy-handed, and often severe. We are doers. Anyone who is not a hard-driving production-minded performer is a lazy bum. The emphasis on "more" and "better" is built into our cultural aims regardless of our personal likes or dislikes in reference to the action or the product involved. We have "arrived" when we have made an impact on the world, whether it be a change in the lives of others, a warehouseful of products, a trail of corpses, or a new set of boundaries on a map. What happens to the doer in all this is something else again. It is a topic of this book to detail the emptying, the exhausting fate of exclusive peripheral living.

A patient described his function in regard to the world, and his attendant fate, at a moment when the pro and the con of his peripheral mode emerge for him: "To make it, you use tricks—I mean, *I* use tricks. I see them like a suit of sparkling mirrors. Do *you* see them? Look! You can't see through mirrors. You damn well can't look inside. The mirrors keep *you*, you there, and they keep *you* out. And that mirror suit is brilliant. It makes *me* brilliant!" The patient paused, staying with himself. Then, "Hot in here, in this suit—I'm in here, someplace—It's sad, that mirrors can't see...."

THE HARMONY OF BEING AT CENTER

Culturally, the periphery is more familiar to us as a state than what we would like to describe as being at center. At the periphery we do something to effect a change. At center we are simply sentient.

We have an available image in our culture of a do-nothing quietism. It is related to the state of being at center, but it is largely a parody of the non-manipulating, nonperipheral state which is center. We do not know of a good theoretical way of describing the state of being at center, an effort which would in any event be quite meaningless unless the center has been experienced. A strong, lasting form of being at center is *satori*, (in Zen buddhism; Japanese for "sudden enlightenment"), though once again the comparison suffers by referring to a state known to only a few. *Satori* has no survival qualities in our culture and for that reason alone is neither an aim, nor a frequent occurrence in the world we have made here. But we want to know about center because its experiential lack in us is pathogenic. We will describe center as an experience.

A man is climbing the precipitous flank of a mountain. The sheer stone is bluish and brown and monumentally old. There are intricate patches of lichen.

But will my muscles hold out?
In a crag grows a sweet mountain flower, unexpected and rare.
Will that thing support my weight?
Now the view of a waterfall, spume like stars and sound like thunder.
Will I drown or will I break my neck?
And then he clings to an open height which is truly spectacular.
Will I get dizzy or will I black out?

And if any of this goes on much longer he will go to pieces whether he literally lets go and splatters below or whether he takes leave of his senses. All of him is in the service of a brutally basic survival, a particular state of concentration which filters out anything not directly related to the crisis at hand. In this case, as it happens, he makes it. We will now give him a moment. . . .

He has functioned on the periphery. Every object was judged for its use. Every effort was bent on achieving a state which he has not yet attained. In his case, it was all-absorbing crisis behavior. In many cases, it is standardized habit no matter what the circumstances. But now he enters a new state. He takes one more deep breath, he stands up, looking well put together. Perhaps he says, "Ah!"

There is no crisis demanding attention, there is no demand to do or use anything. He is safe. He can now feel the wind for the *feel* of the wind and he can see all of the view around him and let it come to him as it will. He does not have to do anything to anything, but is simply sentient, simply aware of what is. He does not have to judge things for their worth or their danger, he does not have to plot how to attain the next state. He can allow to be and let be. Now he is at his center.

The particular state of safeness which allows us to find and to remain at center may be due to an absence of danger or due to a presence of available strength. The wording does not matter. What matters is that at center we are aware without purpose, and therefore without perceptive distortion. At center we are at rest, not from exhaustion but from flexible balance. Note parenthetically that there is also a balance when in crisis. It is characterized by an almost overwhelming sensation of strain. When at center, balance requires no purposeful effort. It is a balance, you will note, in which an instant reaction to a change in conditions is possible. The eye can focus immediately, attention can concentrate without the disruption of an opposite pull. When at center, there is no attachment which must be broken in order to react elsewhere. When at center the quietistic calm of simply being is not so much a refusal to do anything, or an inability to do something, as it is an awareness of being available to oneself as need be, as will be.

To be at center is clearly not the state of action as obtains at the periphery, when something is done to something else. But it is not inaction. Sentience, awareness—these are states of a particular sort of action. They are not bent on survival, but they are responsive, live states which exist freely when self-preservation is not at stake. This is the act with no need for reward. When at center, the act of love is possible.

The act of hate is not possible at center, because it has a definitive aim of affecting, of changing, of destroying an object. In contrast, the act of love is a giving, an offering, whose aim is reached in its self-expression.

When at center, no conflictual splits operate in the personality. It is true that in a total commitment to a crisis there are no conflictual splits operative either—at the price of a severe reduction in the range of receptivity. In contrast, when at center the perceptive range remains wide.

For the therapist, as well as for anyone else, the state of being at center allows for receptivity and a quiet acceptance. Paradoxes such as neurotic-healthy, mind-body, good-bad, right-wrong all become unnecessary judgments, unnecessary ways of fixing the fluidity of experience. Even the sight of a veritable mess does not compel the man who is at center to pack everything instantly into a row of labeled boxes.

It is therapeutically important to note that the use of a category is a form of distortion. Particularly at early moments of the therapeutic encounter any organizational attempt is a contamination of the encounter. While being at center, there is no self-preservational need to change anything. You can see, and let be.

When at center, value judgments are not needed to safeguard one's own integrity, and therefore one can view what is without the interference of judgments which ordain what ought to be.

We have a term for the ability to see and be in touch, without judgment. We call it impersonal empathy. The regard for the other is impersonal in the sense that self-support or personal status is not at stake. The regard is empathic because a relationship is possible which not only respects the integrity of the other but is accepting of the other with no terms imposed. To be at center then means to be in a state of nonjudgmental awareness, or—in the phrase we coined—to have impersonal empathy.

For the therapist, impersonal empathy allows for the view of the patient on his own terms and permits for action which does not depend on the patient's approval. At center, with impersonal empathy, the therapist sees more of what exists because the screening devices of autism from the inside and moralizing from the outside are not called into use. The therapist functions best when he can avail himself of his center. The patient no longer needs his therapist when he too can avail himself of his center.

We are not suggesting a higher value for center than for periphery. We only stress the center state and its harmonies because there is a conventional premium placed on the qualities of the periphery. The contemporary pathology of the periphery is the difficulty of getting rid of it. The pathology of the center is the difficulty of finding it.

Our descriptions of center may suggest a necessary modicum of indifference in that state, but it is not indifference which we would contrast with the involvements of actions and feelings at the periphery. We think of detachment. When at center, you know that we are all brothers under the skin, but also that you are in your own skin and not in his. If this skin-sense of identity, so to speak, disappears, then the therapeutic encounter is one of identification. You feel what the patient feels and you tend to react as the patient will. The therapist, having lost his impersonal empathy, is now in a state of shared distortions with the patient. This condition of confluence, of respective loss of identity, contradicts the very meaning of encounter. An oceanic feeling belongs to events of tremendous merging, which is quite the opposite of finding one's identity. The confluence of the orgastic release belongs with the lover, not the therapist. When confluence and personal attachment arise in the therapeutic encounter, then those moments become centerless and devoid of any differential awareness. There is no exchange. There is no I-Thou relationship.

One patient who discovered his center after relinquishing his identification with the therapist spoke of his new discovery with a slight touch of apology for being disloyal: "You can assess whatever you want out of it, and it's not like I'm cutting myself off from you, but it's really true that this detachment from you is my individuality. Now I know people prize you—I mean, it's not like I don't recognize your worth, but it's now the only way that I can, in a sense, assert *my* self. By standing off, I sit here and look at you now and, so help me, I do enjoy your presence."

The proneness for being out of touch and not knowing it, the difficulty of regaining existential awareness, this potential for losing the sense of center is our potential for sickness. In this sense the entire psychotherapeutic process is the work that it takes to move from the periphery to the center. It is true that the more we are engaged with a crisis the less we are at center. It is also true that the less we are at center the more apt will we be to experience any event as a crisis. The pathologic progression then becomes cyclic and vicious. We remain at the periphery so as to cope with crises, and the more we harden into habitual periphery functions the more unrelieved does the crisis experience become. What, in the end, is *not* a crisis for the neurotic? Only his center, which he no longer knows. . . .

CONDITIONING AND CHARACTEROLOGY

Character traits are the relatively automatic behavior patterns which carry an individual through any situation in a characteristic style. Regardless of the new demands of a situation, the man of character responds in predictable and established ways—as if the new situation were already experienced, as if old learning were sufficient for the new. In that sense character traits are based on fiction.

By responding in habitual ways we economize on the effort involved in making new and unique responses. And we also close ourselves to the present moment. Repetitive reinforcement, either positive or negative, may fix an individual's present responses so that their conditioned nature forces a chronic state of responding predominantly out of the past while ignoring the present.

Now the past obscures the present, the newness of life is transformed to routine, and the excitement of the existential encounter is changed to the dissatisfaction of boredom. There are many examples which reveal the genesis of this neurotic self-confinement within lifeless habits. A mother responds to her adult children as if they were still helpless babes. Maintaining a relationship which is now a fiction, this mother does not even know what her children have become. Within the confines of her fiction she feels genuinely chagrined when she is not consulted, when she gets less than the full attention of a dependent child, when she does not get frequent visits, telephone calls, letters to prove that she is being missed. The shallowness and inanity of such communications are only apparent to the child who has now become an adult. To the mother they serve as marginal proofs that nothing has really changed since the days when her satisfactions were genuinely based on a here-and-now experience with her dependent children.

It is one of the tasks of the therapist to help dissolve the conditioned fixity of the patient's character so that the individual can find the satisfactions available in the present, instead of living on the starvation diet of fictions that try to recreate what no longer exists.

This sense of starvation in the neurotic, this chronic dissatisfaction with the little bit of the world he allows to filter toward himself, all this is maintained by the very agency which keeps a habit intact. This is the pathogenic device of desensitization.

To maintain a habit it is necessary to ignore new behavioral demands, to reaffirm that the fiction is the same as the present reality. That takes a lot of leaving out. It requires a reduction in sensitivity to what is actually there. Any area of desensitization in a patient's personality is prime material for psychotherapeutic work. That work must answer the neurotic's complaint that he cannot feel anything.

An individual's characterology is made up of a complex pattern of desensitizations, and every desensitization results in a distortion of the here-and-now, in a reduction in the individual's growth. The original impetus for survival which has occasioned the desensitization has outlived its usefulness when the maintenance of the device habitually warps the individual's contact experience in the present.

The genesis and the denouement of a desensitization finds numerous illustrations. A child has a nagging, complaining mother. To save himself from her constant intrusion the child learns not to listen. This is a positive achievement whose benefits are insured with an increasingly more habitual desensitization. The obliging conditioner is the mother. Every time she opens her mouth, down comes the curtain of desensitized hearing. And why not, since the reward is peace? When the success of the conditioned habit is made socially acceptable by a well-simulated appearance of attentive interest, this individual is now ready to go forth and meet further unpleasant-nesses in the safety of his isolation. He sits in the therapist's office and talks. Next, he listens with a skillful stance of charmed interest. He has heard himself, and it was pretty clever stuff. He does not hear the therapist, because what the therapist has to say might turn out to be positively hateful.

Please note that desensitization is to the receptors what repression is to the effectors. Repression of an impulse—the interruption of an *expression*—is the equivalent event to insensitivity, the interruption of an *impression*. The two functions complement each other. The child who does not hear the mother enhances his ability to suppress, then repress, his anger reaction to her assault. He achieves the dead peace of not even knowing that he would like to strike his assailant.

When therapeutic intervention begins to revive desensitized areas of his personality, there is invariably a loosening of repressions. The patient experiences the dangerous burgeoning of unacceptable wishes. He begins to know all of him a little bit more.

At this point we want to note only briefly that our therapeutic aim of reviving impulse expression is not the same thing as advocating that an impulse be followed through to its untrammeled conclusion. How a wish to kill is handled includes some realistic considerations besides bloodlust. Our emphatic point is this: Before knowing what to do with a feeling it must be known that it exists. The therapeutic transformation of the repressed goes through careful stages: (1) to let oneself *have* the feeling; (2) to be able to *express* it; (3) not being *compelled* to express it; (4) and to *let go* of it. We only mention the steps at this point because they are part of character work. How the steps can be taken will develop as the book progresses.

CONTACT AND WITHDRAWAL

The biological rhythm for action and inaction is waking and sleeping. The complementary rhythm in the psychological organism is *contact and withdrawal.*

To be in contact simply means to be in touch. Unfortunately for our penchant to see simple blacks and whites, we can be *more* or *less* in contact. The less in touch we are, the more we are withdrawn. The purpose of this child's game with words is rather serious. Our built-in complexity, our versatility, if you will, makes it possible for us to be in contact on the cognitive level, for example, but not necessarily anywhere else. I know intellectually that my act was hostile. However, I did not feel the hostility. We will call full contact the state when our sensitivity allows for a felt echo in our emotions as well as for a comparable impression on the intellectual faculties. In other words, we want to say more about contact than to call it the state of being in touch. Good contact is to be in touch all over. Contact at its best is cognitive awareness with feelingful experience.

While we are about this dissection business of our receptor capacity, we will show our view on how we think we know anything. We regard the intellectual capacity as a scanning device. It scans what we feel. If we feel nothing, then there is nothing to scan, and any intellectual application is useless. (Such intellectual activity does have a use for its own sake. It is called *intellectual exercise,* or—when applied to a phantom problem which is treated as if it were a present event—*mental gymnastics.*)

From the point of view of the therapist, the working emphasis on feeling something through is not a paean to extol emotion over intellect, or feeling over understanding; it is simply a matter of practical necessity. In our cultural context the neurotic is invariably the individual who pays for his particular form of balance with a topheavy emphasis on intellectual agility and a reduced permissiveness for the motion of feelings. As their brains bulge, their guts shrivel. The less they feel, the less burdened is their fanciful dance with the meaningless. The delights of such freedom have their limits. If all this worked well, there would be nobody in the therapist's office.

From the practical point of view the first sine qua non of psychotherapy is to help the patient feel again. Paradoxically, this includes the patient who complains of feeling too much. Briefly stated, his case is not a question of feeling too much but of overreacting. His complaint is real, but his diagnosis is false. His problem comes down to the same complaint which the anesthetized patient has: he does not feel differentially. All is one murk, whether there is too much feeling or too little. While this patient may know himself intellectually, the knowledge is useless unless he, the object of his contemplation, can feel or experience that he is really there. The physical experience of the body image must become whole again. The void of desensitized areas must again be filled with presence, and the emotional experience of possessing a feeling must again become permissible. The assault of an emotion (a threat for the anesthetized patient, a defeat for the one who "feels too much") must again become an expression of his own strength which comes out of him instead of remaining a disowned strength which then assaults him.

Characteristically we fluctuate from contact to withdrawal and back again in a kind of life-rhythm. But in our concern for potential pathology, we must remember that this very flexibility of our rhythm gives leeway to choice. Our concern here centers on the choice of specific withdrawals, i.e., resistances, desensitizations, scotomas. Their nonrhythmic fixity are the clue to the patient's intent. I choose not to become aware and I implement that particular choice with the total excellence of my intellect, which will guarantee my continued ignorance.

The underdeveloped ability to integrate feelings produces the compulsive patient's harsh decrees of control. The compulsive's annihilation of feelings keeps him away from precisely the subject matter of his complaint—his chaotic feelings. It is the therapist's paradoxical task to help the patient turn again to the very experience of his anguish. To help the patient feel again involves the feeling of pain. It may well be the prime fiction of patients in our culture that they assume pleasure will be theirs again, but never pain. They want heaven, not earth.

It is in the very nature of the blind and automatic safety which resistances supply that a patient cannot will himself to get better. But he can work to get better. The degree of his willingness to pay attention to the painful symptom is an indicator of his chances for success in psychotherapy. There is no such thing as an unwilling psychotherapy. Psychological changes imposed by threat, bribe, or wheedling are changes which the patient makes without his personal commitment. In such a case patient and therapist work together not cooperatively but coercively. Brainwashing is one example of this approach, and it succeeds in making psychological alterations. But brainwashing is not psychotherapy, whose aim is to regain the freedom to commit and implement flexible choices, not to acquire a specific conviction or performance.

To stimulate the patient's willingness to work through pain, to offer help without the jeopardy of undercutting the other one's own effort, to offer him strength without dependence—that is the ever-changing and the delicate requirement of therapeutic work.

There are limits to what can be done therapeutically. They are those of the patient and those of the therapist. These limits of capacity must be known by both parties in the therapeutic encounter. Within the respective capacities of patient and therapist exists freedom of choice—the quality that makes one personality uniquely different from the other. Any attempt to operate beyond such limits results in the gamut of illusions from omnipotence on the part of the therapist to paradisiac security on the part of the patient.

It is the very special nature of the therapeutic situation that one of us comes for help to the other, but that the more helpless one must not be deprived of personal responsibility. Without this knowledge, neither the patient nor the therapist succeeds.

RESPONSIBILITY AND BLAME

In our usage the term *responsibility* means the willingness to accept the consequences of an act, or the nature of a condition, as something with which we will deal—*regardless* of whether the condition originated from us or from outside ourselves.

To convey the full significance of our therapeutically oriented meaning we will need more than a definition. We will therefore argue the point and then illustrate it.

Consider that in the prevalent mood of cause-and-effect thinking we will instantly look for the source of trouble when we are confronted with an event that we do not like. Consider also that in a cause-and-effect context we can always find that multiple causes (sometimes called multiple determination) have contributed to the event under scrutiny. If you have any doubts about the wisdom of committing yourself to a present impasse and its consequences, then the facts of multiple determination will always give you leeway to decide that this onerous mess has not been your fault, but the fault of circumstances beyond your diligent control—that George did it and therefore, by God, let George pay for it.

Examples in the therapeutic situation are legion. A patient has reached an impasse with his wife and each critical encounter heralds a violent headache. The wife, demonstrably, happens to be a shrew. Conclusion? That shrew gives me a headache. The same reasoning, utilizing all the leeway of probabilities that are built into situations of multiple determination makes executive pressures responsible for an ulcer, makes a punitive father responsible for frigidity, makes the perfect mother responsible for impotence, and may even leave enough room to discover after five years of psychotherapy that Aunt Julia was really the cause of it all.

Responsibility, as we described it, has now been altered into blame. Responsibility delegated *is* blame. I blame, instead of taking on a task. I justify, instead of altering a condition. I remove myself from actively entering a situation, instead of staying with it and facing its consequences.

The stance of blame obviates action. The patient is safe from all the risks attendant on the leap into the altered situation and its newness.

From an existential point of view the source of a problem is not of first importance. In fact, the job of tracing may be a purely academic issue. Instead, the emphasis of interest is on the impasse as it exists now: What is the manner of the individual's encounter?

The wife who "causes" the headache does not have the headache. You have the headache. It is your headache and what are you doing with it? And if the cause of your distress is your dead mother, a consequential attitude of blame will automatically make cure impossible. Obviously, the dead are not going to rise for action.

To become aware of the difference between responsibility and blame is sine qua non for progress from neurotic stasis toward participation in the movement of living again. Any time the patient feels that something else must change before he can get well (or will take action), his attitude is one of blame, his prognosis one of zero. Instead of committing himself to the risk and promise of change he stays intimate with blame which will give birth to her two monster children, resentment and guilt.

When blame produces no results, resentment follows. Its rankling reiterations are the substitute for action. When blame is turned against oneself, its offspring is guilt, as useless and as never-ending in its agony as anger, resentment, or rage.

The therapist's task is clear: no quarters can be given to the delay in responsible action which comes from blame. And at this point of the therapeutic impasse the therapist's mettle gets it basic test: can he support the patient, who is wavering in pain and anguish, without taking on the other's responsibility and thereby, once again, become the substitute for the patient's own commitment to responsibility?

THE POSSIBILITIES OF CHANGE

The aspects of the personality which are concerned with defending, manipulating, judging, appraising, assigning values, and of sorting the world into the good and the bad, we have called the *periphery*. Then we described the center. When at center the view is existential. The emphasis is on what is, not on what ought to be. The contemplative eye moves over varied dimensions, instead of focusing only on value or usefulness. In short, when at center there is no struggle to gain, to get rid of, to attract, or to repel. The only rhythm is one of interest in the object's own dimensions. This view from the center is the only one whose breadth includes more than one value system, more than the limits of defensive safety, more than the shrunken sight of blame. When the therapist is at center he can recognize without rejection, without judging all the varieties of strange, familiar, nauseating, appetizing, stupid, or insidious devices of self-preservation to which he will be exposed.

And that includes his own.

The therapist has his own beliefs, and his own values. But when at center, and as a therapist, he does not attempt to impose them on anybody else. The patient, just as clearly, is entitled to his own value system. The therapist does not determine what is right or wrong, but he finds out what is; and he helps the patient to find out the same.

The values by which a person lives determine the choices he will make. (Sartre has said that value is choice.) The gain for the patient at that point—assuming he allows the transition from blame to responsibility—is to learn the obvious: to take the consequences of the choices which he makes.

There is no therapy as long as the patient only asks advice. There is no therapy when the therapist decides for the patient what he ought to do.

When functioning from his center, the therapist, in possession of himself and free to contact his existential situation, is now capable of what we mentioned as impersonal empathy. He can respond without the need to force an alteration. He can appreciate the other's suffering and respond with the unique human warmth which gives only itself, and which in this uniqueness supports without resorting to judgments. The therapist recognizes the patient's plight, but does not join in his blame. He attends to the complaint, but does not join the patient's own and unique defenses. As with Martin Buber's I-Thou relationship, neither participant loses his own identity. If the therapist joins the patient to the extent of identification—making the other's pain his own, merging his view with that of the other—and then acts as if there were no separate identities, therapy has once more ceased. Then misery has not only sought company, but has found it. The nonjudging view is lost, and all becomes a mire of shared blame, hate, and a rabbit hunt for ultimate and unattainable causes. The patient's stasis has been perpetuated.

The temporary relief via identification has pushed off the task of engaging in the painful encounter of the resistances whose function it is to ward off change. But to build something new in the personality, something old must be destroyed. And whenever a resistance gives way, there is suffering.

God knows patients suffer enough without therapy, but with a difference. Their characteristic suffering is meaningless. These are not the birth pangs of alteration but the cramps of stasis. The patient's suffering leads nowhere until it is altered to meaningful suffering.

We therefore distinguish between the pain of holding a cramp, so to speak, and of dissolving a cramp. It might be well to let the spooky patient know of this difference in quality, this meaningful difference in end results. Whether he then commits himself to the temporary pain of growth versus the perpetual pain of holding still is dependent partly on the capacity of the therapist to stay at center and attend, and mostly on the choice of the patient.

You show him the meaningfulness of responsibility, and he learns to bear his pain. You help him dissolve his anguished marriage to blame, and he learns to forgive. You give him the calm warmth from your center, and he will attempt the new.

chapter 2

The Starting Experience

THE PLACE OF THE PATIENT'S HISTORY

Before active work toward change can begin the therapist wants to know the patient. Meanwhile, the patient wants to know about the therapist, about himself, about the nature of treatment, about diagnosis, about prognosis, and also about the sounds from the street which suggest a possible traffic jam. The patient clearly faces the more pressing welter of problems.

This is a sensitive time, a time when the patient is least equipped to deal with sensitive matters. The patient's attempts to find safety in shallow waters will now begin to show. The tendency will persist, and this entire book deals with ways of moving from impersonal talk to personal touch and encounter.

In the context of the starting experience it is most often the recording of a case history which the patient will use to talk about things that are distant. He is now apt to remove himself from a present encounter with himself and the therapist. For this reason alone we suggest that history taking be kept rather short. In addition, any extensive cataloguing of chronologies tends to give the beginning patient the idea that therapy is a question-and-answer game, that it is all about past events, and that such items of history are responsible for his present plight. In this sense he will function less as a participant in his own problems and more like someone playing hide-and-seek in an attic.

There are facts to be found which deal with the patient's becoming, but it is a common mistake to become so involved in "getting the facts" that the patient may get lost in the process. There are innumerable items that can be listed about any individual and innumerable causal events that pertain to the patient's present situation. Every organism functions as a whole. Therefore any aspect of his history affects in some manner his present condition. Everything is relevant. In that generalization lies the danger of never coming to grips with this particular patient at this particular time.

But we will take the patient's history in order to obtain an initial view of the nodal events which the patient considers important. We will not argue about his selections. Their respective weights will develop later. For the moment we ask directly about the course of his family life—the events in his life that he finds memorable. But as suggested before, any pursuit in detail at this early time will most likely produce a pile of facts, fancies, and fabrications large enough to hide a full-grown patient.

We have learned this: If the interviewer uses the compiling of a history as a way which helps to *describe* the patient's present situation, then he is not so apt to stray away from the point of his inquiry, which is this patient. In contrast, when the therapist embarks on an archeological expedition in search of explanations the ensuing web of possibilities can become monstrous. We suggest that the history is viewed as descriptive information which then becomes the ground against which the patient's present functions stand in relief.

The difference between a descriptive and an explanatory orientation in the gathering of material from the patient resides not in the telling of the history, but in the use to which it is put. For example, a 30-year-old male patient gave his presenting complaint as irritability with superiors, repeated situations in which the patient felt victimized, and general inability to cope with his karma of an unfair life. Even our initial meandering over points of his past showed the pattern of resentment that was dogging the patient. The historical onset of the patient's attitude of resentment was a childhood relationship with an older brother. There seemed objective cause for resentment. The older sibling was favored with better brains, better muscles, and superior charm.

So far this history is either descriptive, or explanatory. We will use it for both purposes and then note the results.

As an explanation this history now saddles us with the unmanageable task of having to talk away an event in the past which is the putative explanation for a present condition. That is not therapy because the causal event is not accessible to manipulation. It is past.

In contrast, history as a description of the patient's behavior has identified the pattern of his complaint. We have described his unfinished business from the past. The agitation of the past engagements with the patient's brother is perpetuated in resentment (he has not forgiven the sibling), and he is ipso facto living with an unfinished situation. It colors his present, it alters his capacity for encountering new events. We have now described his present mode of behavior, and that is accessible to therapeutic work.

Every patient we have known has carried with him the baggage of several major, unfinished relationships and incompleted situations. These are the main weights which prevent him from standing up straight in his present life. It is the purpose of the history to help identify these burdens.

Historical integration as we have described it is best served by the open-ended question, not by the request for specific, factual detail. A cookbook prescribing the ingredients which you need for a particular stew will give you that stew. Whether it has anything to do with the stew in which the patient finds himself cannot be learned from the book but only from your patient.

You do not prescribe his make-up for him. You follow him. This is as true for the first session as for the last. It is as true for the time when you gather his history as for the time when active changes occur. In each event the patient will present you with the essential aspects of his mode of functioning if he is given the chance. That mode is the way in which he lives now. A history for its own sake is irrelevant for the psychotherapeutic process. Its focus, its length, and its detail are only relevant as they add to the description of the patient's present plight. Therefore what we here mention last comes first in the initial session: much description by the patient of what has brought him here, why he thinks he is here; and from the therapist, much listening.

WHAT IT MEANS TO MAKE A DIAGNOSIS

A diagnosis formulates how the patient is currently functioning. The diagnostic description contains his motivations and his customary patterns of responding.

Whereas the descriptions came from the patient, the diagnosis comes obviously from the therapist. Frequently, the "presenting problem," the patient's complaint, is not the patient's "real problem" at all. Directly or more indirectly the presenting problem relates to the real one. The complaint, for instance, is a headache. It is at best a sympton, a reaction, if you will, to the conflict situation which produces it. In this case, as an example, the real problem is a sustained condition of hostility which is kept under chronic control. The diagnosis must distinguish between and include both the presenting and the real problem, and must further show how they are at this point assumed to be related. In general, a new patient is not able to give a thorough description of his problems and will learn only in the course of therapy how to experience them fully. Without such widened contact with himself he can of course not give a full description.

An essential aspect of the diagnostic formulation is to state how the unfinished business from the patient's past affects his present functioning. Only when it is known what is unfinished will it be known what needs to be done.

The therapist may see what is needed as early as the first session, but it is a practical fact that this knowledge is either inaccessible to the patient or would serve to disturb him further. The chief reaction of a patient to confrontation with his difficulties is anxiety, and to introduce anxiety before a solid relationship has been established will only tend to chase the patient away.

Instead, it is important in the first session that the patient feels he is being understood. Interpretations or diagnostic material from the therapist do not serve this end. They may enhance the therapist's image of instant competence, an item which gives proof of his superiority. It may frighten the patient with the revelation of his conflict, an item which gives proof of his inferiority. If this should occur, then the detrimental dependency relationship will only have to be worked out in the later course of therapy, an added chore which therapist and patient can well do without. The diagnosis is designed to answer one basic question: What are the phenomena of the patient's existence—what makes him a patient? Here we look at the constructs that shape his life, the fictions by which he lives. They shelter him and they support him. These hallowed fictions are guarded with blessed blindness and any diagnostic exposure at the rate of the therapist's insight can be painful and shattering to the beginning patient.

The diagnosis is for the therapist. His written account may well take any form which is most meaningful to him. The therapist's creative touch in the description of behaviors will vary, but we see in any event no need to restrict oneself to the relatively small repertoire of classic psychiatric terminology. For example, to say that a patient has an insatiable-leech syndrome may prove to be much more evocative than the standard jargon, such as "oral-dependent type." The nuance of an impression made by a patient can be lost by the purely arbitrary restriction to a clinical vocabulary. A young man who was passive-dependent with pronounced masochistic characteristics sounded very much like a thousand others who suffer demonstratively; but this one came alive again in the notes which said that he had a "bleeding-Jesus" syndrome.

What is generally communicated with this sort of statement is drawn from our veritable storehouse of richly associative stereotypes. What they lack in computer precision they make up in unusual richness. We would consider any device legitimate which does the best job of capturing the quality of the patient.

But back to the patient in his first session. He will ask whether the therapist really thinks there is something wrong. Suffice it to say that the patient would not be there if he did not think so, and the therapist would not accept him into treatment if he did not agree. If a relationship of worth is to develop, let it be started with openness instead of evasion.

Without resort to interpretations, the patient, as we have discussed, can certainly be told that there is something wrong. If the patient is concerned about the severity of his problem, the answer can again be direct. Telling the patient that he seems indeed seriously disturbed can only be troublesome if the therapist feels hostile in the face of the problems he sees. If his answer comes from a basis of understanding instead of rejection, then the troubled patient can recognize that he has now found someone who wants to help him toward health. Many patients are relieved to hear the therapist admit that he too sees a problem. These patients have had their complaints belittled or minimized by casual friends and by anxious relatives. That sort of hollow support is not therapy. Directness in this regard is often the starting point of trust in the therapeutic relationship.

Until now we have discussed the making of a diagnosis as if the therapist were a disinterested observer or an inactive recipient of information. Such a degree of personal detachment might be welcomed by the patient, if he had come to have his fingerprints taken. In that case, the less personal the better. But he has come to another human being for help.

In general, informality and a personable attitude are the best start for a meaningful relationship. The instrumental moments of diagnosis occur for the therapist when he is in touch with and allows himself to be affected by the patient's existential situation. The therapist will only be able to understand the patient's position if he is able to let himself be "touched" by the patient. Once again, we speak of the state of impersonal empathy. And once again the point is delicate: We are decidedly not talking about identifying with the patient.

It is possible to put yourself into the patient's shoes without becoming the patient. It is possible to experience the patient's situation as he would, but without being the patient.

The aspect of the therapist which becomes identified with the patient is no longer available for the therapeutic encounter. The therapist's usefulness is proportionately reduced. Where there is identification, there is shared distortion! Where there is shared distortion, the therapeutic encounter does not exist.

THE QUEST FOR INSTANT PROGNOSIS

Both patient and therapist have a critical—if not too critical—interest in prognosis from the start. From the therapist's point of view, the question is practical: How well can I work with this person and what are the chances of success? In this connection it is important to estimate the patient's motivation for treatment.

The more the patient wants to change, the better the prospects. But the most telling criterion for prediction is the patient's readiness to suffer the roughness of it. The therapist may well have to make clear from the outset that therapy is not easy and will not always be fun. The patient must know that there will come periods of distress and anxiety, but also that such a turn in events need not disappoint him.

The patient who accepts this prediction gives the best prognosis. While many may wish with all their hearts to change for the better, a goodly number of them do not intend to run the risk of trying something new or unknown. Prognosis: Doubtful.

We have not met the patient who has not some degree of doubt, some moments of anxiety about his chances of improving. He may not mention this, but we think it appropriate that the therapist answer him, if he asks.

In general, the gain from therapy is proportionate to the effort devoted to it. But the therapist can be more to the point and state honestly what his estimate for improvement is, adding that this estimate is only an educated guess. As the therapist cannot guarantee success, neither can he guarantee failure.

It is likely that the patient will ask how long his therapy will take. Since this cannot be predicted with any useful reliability, the therapist must not offer any quantitative guesses. But then it may or may not come as a surprise to the therapist that some patients have no idea whatsoever about the length of psychotherapeutic treatment. In that case this general topic might well be discussed.

It is not uncommon that a patient becomes reluctant to get involved at all once he learns that there are no guarantees, and once he is told that treatment can last months or years. When the therapist recognizes such doubt in the course of the first session, it is good procedure to suggest to the patient to refrain from deciding for or against therapy now. It is better to ask him to go home, think about it, and not make up his mind for a week. Then he should tell the therapist what he has decided. If the patient is reluctant in the first session and decides to enter therapy after a week's thought, then he is likely to make a more solid commitment whan therapy starts.

But the therapist may feel reluctant himself. The same resistances which harness the patient operate on him also.

It is not good practice to work with a patient with whom the therapist feels hopeless. The feeling will surely communicate to the patient and reinforce his own sense of alienation. It is by far the best practice to refer the patient in the very first session to another therapist if it is foreseen that work with the particular patient might entail a great deal of difficulty. The therapeutic encounter is not the proving ground for abilities which are held in doubt.

THERAPEUTIC PLANS AND GOALS

Generally, the patient comes with a complaint and he wants to rid himself of it. If he has overt symptoms that he can define, the goal is the removal of that specific bother. But with increasing frequency a new breed of patient comes for psychotherapy. The symptoms lack easy definition and instead require generalized terms and lofty abstractions: pervasive feelings of loneliness, estrangement, alienation, sense of loss. The intensity of discomfort is as acute as if the complaint were allergy to cotton, but the goals for therapy are as vague as the descriptions of the complaint.

The goals of the therapist who has a patient with specific symptomatology are frequently quite different from the patient's expectations. Both want to get rid of the symptom, but there can be a vast difference about the expectations of method. While the patient may only be concerned with the disappearance of the symptom, the therapist invariably must grapple with the conflicts which generate the symptom.

"I didn't come here for all kinds of yak about that bastard I had for a father. I want to stop being scared of snakes!"

Clearly, the therapist is running into resistance, and that precisely when he is right on target.

Whether the patient has specific or vague complaints, the therapist always tends to pursue more general goals than the patient has contemplated. We have discussed them in the first chapter. They are such goals as increased experiential awareness, a more fully available, integrated personality, and a willingness to risk facing the newness of life as it comes. It might seem that such goals are more appropriate for the patient with *Weltschmerz* and with that all-over feeling of blah; however, we think that they apply just as seriously to the patient whose only complaints are the snakes in his life.

We have a rule of thumb which is good for the initial sessions: The patient comes to obtain what he lacks in himself.

The entire point of the diagnosis is to learn what precisely this particular patient lacks. For example, the patient complains that he feels inadequate, overtaxed, and inferior. As a diagnostic summary we say that he lacks self support.

The diagnosis implies that he will spend his life looking for support from others. He will persistently maneuver for approval from others, because approval—or better yet, praise—can fill the void where his self-esteem is lacking.

However, since he lacks *self*-support, and all he gets is the support of others, clearly his manipulations can never fill the bill. He lacks the feeling of "I am alright," and instead he blindly works for "Let them think I am alright." When he is censured his state of no support is reinforced. When he is praised, he is getting sound but no substance.

Now that the therapist sees the lack in the patient he can approach him with knowledge. He cannot allow himself to approve or to disapprove of his patient, since in either event he would reinforce what is precisely the patient's lack and complaint. Though the patient may remain blind to his essential lack for some time, the therapist now works only to create those moments which require or which can evoke self-support. To instruct with the fiat, "You must show self-support" is as useless as shouting at a deaf man. If he hears you he might even be clever enough to say, "So what. I haven't got any."

Only the experience of actually having strength can alter the conviction that strength comes only from the outside.

THE ENCOUNTER WITH PARADOX

Beginning with the earliest sessions both patient and therapist will encounter emotions which are mutually exclusive but exist side by side. This is the paradox. It owes its existence to the sort of concept which says that when you love, you are incapable of hate. Love and hate are defined as mutually exclusive, which makes for a certain type of clarity in logic. Phenomenologically, this is nonsense.

To experience opposite emotions is a paradox only on the basis of the purification to which we have subjected the terms which cover emotions. In that sense, to encounter the paradox is to engage in battle with a straw man. Nevertheless, there it is.

We have frequently seen the patient who displays great independence in a highly consistent manner. The very extremity of his demeanor and the very consistency of its occurrence may clue us to the fact that we are here dealing with a highly dependent individual. "Methinks he doth protest too much?" And might such consistency smack of the rigid habit which perpetuates itself precisely because it does not take account of changing, existential demands?.

The question is worth exploring and the individual answer will come more easily if we do not worry about the artificial contradiction that dependence and independence exist simultaneously.

As we have suggested, there is no implicit contradiction involved. While dependence and independence can be placed at opposite ends of a linear spectrum of personal qualities, they display aside from their dissimilarity some striking qualities in common: Both are marked with an inflexible insistence on one quality only, both are employed with characteristic and exclusive consistency. We have a helpful *pons asinorum* which makes graphic sense when dealing with opposites: the spectrum with dependence and independence at each end is not linear but curves to approximate a circle. The more extreme the two opposite qualities the closer they will be to each other. They are in fact closer to each other than they are to the midpoint of their spectrum, which adroitly depicts the phenomenon that the dependent person is more likely to jump to the opposite extreme than to find the midpoint of the dependence-independence continuum.

The midpoint—to use the comparison of an extended continuum— may be described in terms of proportions of the extreme, but described in that way we omit its essential quality which distinguishes if from both extremes: At the midpoint there is choice. Flexibility of response is restored. Consistency of reaction is reduced. About this, an immediate comment:

Very frequently young therapists are highly preoccupied with the consistency of their response to a patient. We so not place any great value on such consistency. We find the view of the human being as a machine highly misleading and heuristically useless. In contrast, we do not find it surprising to encounter inconsistencies, paradoxes, and contradictory actions. If the therapist feels and behaves with consistent sameness, it is time to ask himself what the permanent fiction is to which he is responding with machinelike predictability. If, on the other hand, the therapist responds from what is present in the therapeutic encounter, then he will perforce violate the geometric beauty of patterned behavior. Also, he will be alive.

One day, the patient describes intricate reasons which justify his dislike for the watusi. But this is not the therapist's day. He could not care less, he is bored. Perhaps this ought not to be, but it is. If the therapeutic encounter is to remain alive, then it is necessary to engage this foreground phenomenon of boredom between patient and therapist. An insistence on interest which is absent may be the honorable thing to do, but it is also a fake.

But there is a form of consistency which we value: it is to be authentic and open, to respond from the center—which is to say with a *yes* to what is there.

It would be strange indeed, if the therapist were unchanging as he enters an interpersonal world which is extremely complicated, inconsistent, and often chaotic. In the face of such encounters his very consistency would mark him as something apart from life, like an island in the sky. This quality of apartness contradicts the therapeutic requirement of entering the patient's world. Such apartness precludes help.

While the therapist may view the display of inconsistency with a repeated sense of wonder, the patient may be quite unable to accept the phenomenological fact at all. He will, as a patient, be well grounded in what ought to be and may then in proportion refuse to engage with what is. We are not suggesting to therapist or patient that there are no consistent and recurring behavior patterns which may dominate a personality picture, but we make the emphatic point that contradictory beliefs and ambivalent attitudes do not only exist but must be pointed out. And above all, we consider it a mistake to prejudge them as pathological.

Clinicians tend toward the tunnel vision of psychopathology, admitting predominantly the cues of the symptom, the defense, and the pathogenic, unconscious motivation. The emphasis may define the case and leave out the person. The same defect of tunnel vision applies to the therapist who sees only positive growth processes, inherent self-fulfillment tendencies, self-actualization, and —as an old-fashioned echo—brotherly love.

But the rose grows in the dirt.

We attach ourselves to the criteria by which we measure what is important to us. In the therapeutic context, this knowledge gives us a small rule of thumb: Show me your attachments and I will show you your neurosis.

Attachment, when maintained consistently, must move the person to the extremes of his continuum. When personal independence is an issue, the attachment is to the continuum of dependence-independence. The attachment precludes any solutions which do not tend to invoke the full force, the extremes of this preoccupation. Instantly, the individual's flexibility to respond is reduced; in fact, his existential situation has been violated.

Our warning about attachments, our stress on the need to know that they have an effect, is at this juncture especially for the therapist. It is a frequent fact that the therapist who has discovered the feces of the patient will quickly say *no* to that part of the personality. The therapist has now found the demon that he must exorcise, and he sets about with Messianic zeal to rescue the fallen one from his evil.

No one can become free from his attachments—and from his symptomatology—without first saying yes to the attachment. This acknowledgment will then reveal what has been left out. I will gladly proclaim my rosiness—but what happened to my dirt?

Exclusive attachment to particular aspects of the personality is neurotic. That applies to the attachment to Myself the Rose, as to Myself the Filth. But only in affirming both do I have the center.

Unfortunately, forms of attachment are legion: There is one form to the method of how not to become attached, and one form to the ways of how to attain integration—to mention two attractive ones. We mention these because they can occur specifically in the context of psychotherapy. The result is that the fifty-minute hour of therapy becomes more important than life, and the event is exemplified by the frequent patient who lives only for his next session. The compartmentalization of his effort is precisely what undercuts the success of his therapy. His vaunted effort is equivalent to the plan: Today I am going to find God! To which God may well answer: To Hell with you, Brother Stultifas. Today's Sunday and on that day I take a rest, you recall.

OF BASIC INGREDIENTS TAKE LISTENING
AND HEARING

There is no therapy before you hear the patient. Until other techniques are invented, it is necessary to listen, if the patient is to show himself.

Listening is not an easy matter. The room is small, the hours are long, and the talk drones on. Your own fantasies may be much more absorbing.

We have no quick cure for the impasse of not being able to pay constant attention. Perhaps you can, anyway, or perhaps there is no such thing. We do know that it is useless to force a focus of attention, which is equivalent to deciding that persimmons taste like grapes, no matter what. The tour de force can freeze you into insensitivity. But there is the matter of trying it out: What does all this really taste like?

But we were talking about hearing the patient. There is passive listening, where the therapist gives himself over to the wave that the patient sends his way, and there is active listening, which means that the therapist reacts to the patient's output.

The distinction is man-made and we only use it to cast a differential focus. Once having made the point, we would just as soon let the categories go by the board

Passive listening is without any intent to hear something in particular. It allows for the sort of ranging about, for the openness which permits come what may. We think this works well, except that passive listening is without readiness to respond. In that sense, the therapist tends to exclude himself from participation.

Active listening refers to a much more alert searching and hearing. It includes the intent *to hear more than the patient is saying.* As an exclusive intent, of course, you may tend to hear only the thing for which you were listening.

But enough of the categories. We have, in effect, described the indispensable qualities of the way in which the therapist, when at center, listens best. And now for the varied things that he can thus hear. Whenever a person talks he puts forth simultaneous messages on a number of levels. There is the old chestnut in which two therapists pass each other and one says, "How are you?" The other, having read such a book as this, ruminates, *What did he mean by that remark?*

In the therapeutic context, a measure of such sensitivity is in fact required. There is invariably the denotative message: "How are you?", which is a request for designated information. On the connotative level the content of the sample question may mean, "Drop dead." The specific, literal meaning and the implied suggestion may be expressed simultaneously.

A patient asks whether therapist thinks it is going to rain that afternoon. Context may show that the question was a bona fide request for information, a test to ascertain whether the therapist will give a direct answer, a diversion from growing anxiety, and a *volte face*, simply intended to change the subject; any and all such messages may pertain, regardless of topical content.

The therapist may well be aware of several different messages yet be unable to respond to all of them at the same time. He must choose. At best, this choice responds to the patient's dominant intent—and how to decide what that intent is may involve an exchange that goes on until the patient's dominant interest is expressed and checked out.

Unable to provide a rule of thumb, we must here be more discursive. We feel that listening is tantamount to an art. The man without talent for painting will never be an artist. The artist is a man whose ready, unlearned facility for a pursuit draws him to it, provides satisfying expression for him, in high measure allows him to transmit some of the fruits of his gift also to others. The gift can be sharpened, but in itself it cannot be learned. We feel that the ability to listen is very much on that order.

There are many people who are unable to receive the myriad messages that seek reception, whether because of their life experience or their genes. They cannot hear openly without getting swamped by confusion; they may not be able to hear, period, simply because they have a limited range. Theodore Reik has discussed "listening with the third ear" in great detail. Regrettably, he too does not have a training program. But perhaps all you need is to remember some of the characteristics we described for the artist, whose gift draws him to its pursuit, imbues that activity with unique satisfaction, and allows him to impart some of his fruit to another.

But some things in the pursuit of listening are more concrete. To understand listening better we would suggest a distinction between content and style.

The content of spoken words in an exchange is the shared meaning of those words. The style of an exchange is the manner in which it is presented—that is to say, it reflects what the patient is doing in the relationship of the exchange.

The patient discusses his roommate. This is also the most obvious content of his remarks. But his style may be avoidance. For half a dozen sessions he has been dealing with his mother and has come to the verge of discovering his basic distrust of women—then switches to a dissertation on his roommate.

The therapist may be way ahead of this game. He hears avoidance. He cannot ignore it and must respond: "It seems to me you are changing the subject. You are leaving something out. I wonder what it could be?" This response is far better than to follow along with the content which the patient has offered. The therapist is by no means introducing new material by interrupting the patient. Instead, he is responding to what is there. Even though the patient, in this case, was not discussing avoidance, he was most certainly presenting it.

On other occasions the therapist may not know with any degree of clarity at all just what is going on in the interpersonal relationship of that session. The impasse may frequently be resolved by asking for free associations on the content of that moment. Now listen to the patient and not to your personality theory. Now let yourself listen with as little premeditation as you would expect the patient to put into his free associations. Perhaps you need the third ear. You most certainly need the two you have.

There is one other object of attention while listening, and that is the therapist himself. There is an inner voice which has things to say.

At the impasse, at the time of muddle and confusion, it is good to ask, What do I feel now, and what is the patient doing to me?

The therapist is not a carte blanche in the session but an active participant in his own right. By listening to his own reaction the therapist may hear the voice of his own neurosis. If it is there, listen to it and know it for what it is. This knowledge is the hallmark of being a professional. Or this listening to oneself may reveal the patient as he has not been heard before.

One of us once sat with a patient and as if out of the blue became aware of fear. The patient was talking about modern art, a subject that presented no particular threat to the therapist. The therapist turned to his fear and listened. He recognized rapidly that he was afraid of being attacked. At that instant the therapist heard the malevolence in the patient's voice. The content of the conversation was devoid of hostility, but the style was one of insistent threat. With this awareness the therapist could now ask the patient whether he experienced his own aggressive style. In this case, the answer was dramatic. The patient leaped up, smashed his fist on the desk, and vilified the therapist in a sudden, high rage.

The patient's own experience of his mood was now patently unavoidable. It opened the door to a long overdue exploration of this patient's covert aggressiveness. If the therapist had not listened to himself, the conversation might still be on the merits of somebody else's art.

The therapist who cannot listen is no therapist at all. Once he hears, however, he still has not served his full function. Now he must learn how to respond.

THE THERAPEUTIC RESPONSE

We will describe three modes of responding to the patient. They are interpretation, reflection, and confrontation.

Interpretation means that we take what the patient presents, restate it in the light of our theory, and then give it back to the patient in altered form.

The patient describes his need to arrange the top of his desk and the contents of its drawers in painstaking ways. Unless he goes through this meticulous organization of his work space, he cannot possibly do his job in peace.

A moment's academic perusal and we've got it: This patient goes through a compulsive maneuver whose object is control. He must be trying to master some loathesome impulse.

If the response to the patient is interpretation, we then clear up everything by telling him what he does not want to know: You have some hidden impulses which you think are so awful they have to be harnessed and controlled by rigid organization.

While diagnostically astute, the response is therapeutically useless.

An interpretation is based on suppositions about the nature of personality. It is as applicable to your compulsive patient who comes at ten in the morning as to your compulsive patient who comes at four in the afternoon. In that sense, the interpretation addresses both of them in general but neither of them in particular. An interpretation will therefore come off as a theoretical statement, whether it is phrased in theoretical language or not.

The purpose of an interpretation is to increase the knowledge about the self. In most insight-oriented schools of therapy interpretation plays a very large role. Insight, in this instance, is intellectual knowledge. In contrast, when a psychotherapy is geared toward expanded experiential awareness, then interpretation is an obstacle as frequently as it is an aid.

Interpretations with a small affective component turn out to be intellectual statements which are difficult to relate to a personal experience. In that sense, they tend to encourage intellectualization in the patient, attendant with all the detachment of examining something in a bottle. This facility of viewing oneself *in vitro* instead of *in vivo* undercuts the very purpose of therapeutic redintegration, namely the capacity for again being able to say: This is *I* and not *it*.

It is of critical importance that the therapist know what effect and function an interpretation will have. In general, the more theoretically oriented the interpretive response, the less useful it is for the patient who must learn to be aware of what he really feels.

Can he experience an ego-superego conflict? Can he feel oedipal strivings generating anxiety in regard to mother figures? None of these is an experiential event. At best these abstractions will increase his knowledge of personality theory and at worst he will learn a new jargon. Neither will help him much in his personal growth. Even in the case of less theoretically oriented interpretations it is of vital importance not to furnish the patient with new and sacred devices which aid and abet his depersonalization.

An interpretation must take the patient to the next step of awareness—when he is ready for it. If he is not ready for meaningful assimilation, he will let you know: he will adopt the interpretation without effect. Like Faust, after years of study he will feel as stupid as he was before.

By and large, interpretation plays a minor role in center psychotherapy, and lest (again like Faust) the patient sign himself over to a pact worse than the one with his therapist, let us try another method of response.

When the therapist acts like a simple mirror for the patient than he practices reflection. He feeds back what the patient is putting out. Carl Rogers has made reflection the chief technique of his nondirective method when it was first developed. He makes the important point that the therapist can reflect feeling as well as the tone content, both of which come to him from the patient. The distinction is of considerable practical importance. We have found that reflecting only content has little if any effect on the patient, except that it will irritate him.

On the other hand, reflecting the patient's emotional tone can help the patient move closer to what he is actually feeling at the moment and then the exploration of the feeling can become a fruitful focus for work. Instead of responding to the content of what the patient is saying, the therapist can reflect the patient's affect, the very feel of what he is experiencing. But this possible benefit of the reflection technique is much too easily crowded out by a weed that thrives on the method: the therapist's increasing facility with paraphrase. It is an improvement on the method but the chief improvement is with the range of vocabulary.

The constant retranslation of the discourse into alternate verbiage may indeed fascinate or stultify the patient. The paraphrase may mollify. It will most certainly delay action, and that includes any action. It is not designed to provoke a new step because it is no more than a rehash. Only the patient's dissatisfaction with the response by paraphrase may inadvertently egg him on into a new step for the sheer sake of a difference.

Obviously this is not a very efficient way of promoting change, but even if change is produced, its quality is negligible. Consider the function of reflection: it makes known by reiteration how the patient feels, what his behavioral intent is at the moment of inspection. This describes the level on which the technique has an impact, namely the periphery. We have described the periphery of the personality as the aspect of moods, conditioned behavior patterns, reactive feeling, and formation of intent. In brief, the particular experiential state which we have described as center is entirely left out.

Reflection can only reflect. In that sense it can hardly engender anything beyond the scope of the material presented. It cannot point beyond the experiential state that is encountered, and therefore awareness is never broadened beyond the peripheral state.

We have described interpretation and reflection with an emphasis upon their limited usefulness. The limitations were specifically measured in regard to the one imperative requirement of the therapeutic encounter: expanding experiential awareness.

Interpretation expands intellectual facility. The contingent quality of depersonalization may neglect, if not atrophy, the personal experience of the state which interpretation describes.

Reflection focuses on awareness of the periphery, but within all the limits of habit and autism which the particular patient's periphery may contain. The method does not engender the second view, the alternate point of departure, the awareness which lies beyond judgment. Neither method is designed to reach for the center. The act of confrontation without the use of intentional categories, without the distortions of the purposeful focus which resides in all peripheral activity—such clearness without autism and prejudged value is rarely available to these two techniques. The technique of confrontation is our offer toward the main job of the therapeutic encounter, the expanding experiential awareness.

We will have to take back the word *technique*. Confrontation is an approach and a fluid achievement of the very state which it tries to reach: awareness through the act of confronting each other. The characteristic ingredient of confrontation can be gleaned by the qualities which the other two techniques leave out; interpretation operates on an impersonal level, and reflection omits the therapist. Confrontation, on the other hand, is personal in the sense that the therapist reacts to the patient and not to the case; it involves the therapist as a person, in the sense that he respond from his center. The therapeutic encounter which we call confrontation is achieved when the therapist reacts from his center. It is fulfilled when the patient reacts from his center too. The view from the center sees a world which is unaltered by wish, by dream, by projection. Rephrased in the positive, the view from the center sees the world of here-and-now. The therapist who sees the patient in this way and reacts from that basis confronts the patient. And the patient who achieves that confrontation has reached his center.

To the extent that confrontation is a technique, it consists of the repeated referral to an aim: Am I responding with impersonal empathy? Is the patient working toward his center?

Clearly, confrontation does not lift the encounter to a level of theory-oriented manipulations, nor does it function with the impersonality of a mirror. In confrontation the act is between I and Thou. Buber said this for us: "All real living is meeting."

In that sense confrontation becomes a microcosm of life, and to the extent that this confrontive living is achieved, to that extent has the patient transcended the special circumstances of the therapeutic hour.

And to the degree that confrontation is real life, in that same measure does the technique contain its own dangers.

There are risks. They are the same as those away from the session. However, the difference between the microcosm of the session and the macrocosm of the life outside the session is merely that a confronting therapist is present in the one but not in the other.

If the therapist does not react to the patient from his center—in an I-Thou relationship, in fact—then he joins the same unfeeling world from which the patient suffers elsewhere. If the therapist reacts with hostility *qua* hostility, then he confirms precisely what the patient has suspected all along—that the world is against him.

These are some of the risks of confrontation. Let us stay with the kind of encounters subsumed under hostility, since they cover perhaps the widest span of events that are meaningful to a patient.

Here is a patient who drones on and on in a mood of petulance. It may not take long and the therapist becomes mainly aware of his own irritation. If the therapist reacts with some such remark as, "Shut up, I've had it!" then he has reacted from his periphery (with hostility in this case) and the confrontation is nontherapeutic. If, on the other hand, the therapist reacts from his center (with impersonal empathy) then he can say this: "At the moment I can only hear your droning. I feel frustrated with hearing no more than the sound, hammering at me. Let us discuss it." Now the confrontation is concerned with the essence of the encounter. The therapist's hostility is not used against the patient, though it is admitted as a fact. The subject matter of discourse is now the very friction point at which contact is made—the droning assault on one hand, the hostile reaction on the other—and the phenomenological event of that moment is met in confrontation.

The patient must now also confront his own mode of activity. "You are whining like a petulant child," confronts the therapist. "Can you hear it? Listen," and now his actual behavior becomes subject matter, instead of the topical content of his speech. If any of this is pointed out from a sense of irritation, then the therapist's comment is a mere admonition, and once again nontherapeutic. If his concern speaks, if he can feel that he wants to help the patient out of his device of petulance, then a therapeutic effect can again be reached.

Clearly, confrontation frequently points to something that the patient does not want to hear. But the therapist who speaks from his center can touch any topic while the patient still feels that he is being accepted.

In a wider sense than the confrontive event in a session, the patient does not only learn more of himself but can learn to be more confrontive with others. His relationships become more open, more direct, and more honest. His neurotic relationships can diminish as his confrontive ability grows.

Back to the therapist who has his own troubles. This one, in religious adherence to the principles of confrontation, feels that he must say everything to the patient that comes up: what he sees in the patient, what he understands about his dynamics, and exactly how the other one comes across. This man's patient will now get bombed with a wealth or welter of truths, whether the patient is able to assimilate the material or not.

This honest man in the therapist's chair needs to remind himself of only one thing: he is not there to speak for the sake of a therapeutic principle. He is there for the sake of a patient.

We have a rule of thumb for the event of a confrontation. After it is offered we wait to see what the patient does with it. It gives the patient the chance to cogitate and perhaps to assimilate. It shows the therapist whether the patient has been struck in a sensitive spot, reacts with anxiety, and now needs support in the new situation. It goes without saying that support does not take the form of backtracking, but it does mean that the therapist stay with the patient and show him his empathy.

It is true that a confrontive statement by the therapist goes almost invariably beyond the patient's current level of awareness. And that is precisely its function, the expansion of awareness.

In the microcosm of the therapeutic encounter—exemplified by the act of confrontation, made possible by the view from the center—by these can a life be found that is without fear of self-loss, a life full of the knowledge of self-growth.

SOMETHING OF VALUE

The first session is not basically different from any other. Two people confront each other in an effort to work together. The therapist proceeds as he must at any other time: he starts where the patient is at that moment and works from there. As for the patient, he has come for help, for a cure—not excluding a magical one—and to find out what the therapist can do for him. These expectations are the only features that are apt to occur with more concentration in the first session than in later ones. Also, please note we did not say that the patient expects to work. By and large he does not. We do not impute laziness, but we point out that the patient does not know how to work therapeutically, or else he would not have come.

The prevalent expectations of the patient can be met in the first session. Give the patient something of value.

We have found it is very important that the therapist disclose his therapeutic style from the start. We are not suggesting that the therapist run through his repertoire for the sake of demonstration. He is not being auditioned. However, the first session is the beginning of work and it is as much a time of personal encounter as any other.

As for the patient's expectations of cure, there are no guarantees. In most cases this must be pointed out, particularly so if the patient fails to be explicit about the matter. He may be cagey about his expectation, or he may be shy, but in any event he will tend to leave the responsibility as well as the work for improvement to the therapist. Let the therapist offer the patient something else instead: his willingness to work with the patient, his ability to understand his plight. A demonstration of these two qualities alone will in most instances be vastly more than the patient has been getting from any other source, including himself. The therapist does not have to demonstrate that he can resolve the patient's impasse, but he does need to demonstrate that he is bringing something to the session which will produce constructive alterations in the patient's ineffectual style.

All of this will also help to dispel the patient's implicit notion that he is now subject to a magical rite which—in the course of esoteric incantations, chants, and passes—will wreak dramatic rebirths. This particular expectation will not disappear in one session, but the first session is the time to state, if not make clear, that this notion will have to go.

In the place of this myth the therapist must offer himself, his empathy for the patient's plight, his willingness to reach into the cul de sac, his assurance that he will offer what the patient has denied himself—a way to again avail himself of his own strength.

THE GOOD SAMARITAN AND THE GOOD THERAPIST

He gave the shirt off his back and has not been heard of since. So much for the Good Samaritan.

The Good Therapist is the one who does not accept every patient. He chooses the one in whose case he can make a good prognosis. Anything less is not honest, anything more is nonprofessional.

The personal commitment which goes into making a positive prognosis is the very stuff which transmits itself to the patient as the persistent *yes* in the therapist's effort. That is clearly not the same thing as high expectations or glowing promises, both of which are fantasies.

Every therapist works better with some patients than with others, though the reason for this may well remain obscure. In general it is true that the patient with whom the therapist is most ineffective presents areas of psychological difficulties which the therapist himself shares. If the encounter with the patient is too raw, too irritating an aggravation of the therapist's own problem areas, then the therapeutic pace will be heavy-footed and painful indeed. The more aware the therapist is of himself and the sooner he can recommend a therapist better equipped than himself, the better he fulfills his appointed function in this case. If, in contrast, the patient is accepted because he represents a challenge, once again the prognosis is bad. In such a case the patient is used as a foil in the service of the therapist's self-improvement, a thoroughly unprofessional manner of conduct, because the therapeutic situation is not designed as a battleground.

We are not suggesting that the therapist reject patients on the basis of prospective difficulties per se. In general, one of the most difficult problems encountered is the patient with a highly rigid characterological make-up. If the patient does not reflect the therapist's own undissolved problem area in an irritating degree, then the work may well be very hard, but the prognosis can be good. Only if the difficulty of the prospective encounter is implicit in the therapist himself is referral in order.

A variant on this problem of choice is the patient who meshes well with the therapist at the outset, but whose prospective development might present unmanageable problems. Note, for example, the patient whose obsequious and yielding style makes for a productive therapeutic situation. The therapist's residing paternalism works well; his dread of opposition is not provoked. Diagnostically this patient is in need of a belated, adolescent rebellion. Will the therapist be able to cope with it—with himself—once this Jekyll turns into Hyde?

Two more choice points (before the last) which are issues when considering a patient. They are concrete but may be overlooked because their very simplicity is deceptive.

Do you have the time to accept a new patient? It is well to remember that every professional commitment cuts into the time which is available for anything else. And there is no such thing as accepting a case because it is easy, because it is a friend of a friend, not even—harsh thought—because it will bring in more money. Only if the acceptance is solidly in behalf of the therapeutic encounter will the patient gain, will the therapist be worth his salt. Any other consideration per se is not therapy.

But back to the harsh thought. Can the patient pay? If the practice is on a private basis, then the patient's ability to pay the fee is as important as his right to professional help. The matter of fee and the manner of payment must be discussed and made concrete in the first session. It has happened more than once that after a patient has been accepted and a relationship established it develops that the patient cannot pay. At such a point the therapist has the dilemma of living up to his professional responsibility without pay, or breaking his trust in order to get compensation elsewhere. No matter which way that dilemma is resolved, needless resentment, possibly of long duration, can be the consequence.

There remains one instrumental yardstick for acceptance—the patient's reason for entering treatment. Once again the therapist must listen to the patient's explicit and his unverbalized expectations.

The patient wants to learn how to control his sporadic temper. In this case the unverbalized expectation was supplied by innuendoes and mood; the patient wished to be able to express love instead of covering the impulse with screams of hate. The patient was accepted for the stated as well as for an unverbalized reason. The therapist believed he could help with the symptomatic temper problem as well as with the patient's inability to relinquish a love ideal that had long outworn its worth.

The patient's ignorance of the area of work lying ahead is of little moment, particularly if there is evidence that he is *willing* to work. We mention three examples which in contrast suggest a reserved prognosis: the captive patient—the one who has been sent, nagged, threatened, or otherwise dispatched into therapy with a minimum of volition on his own part; the patient who goes into therapy because in his subculture it happens to be the thing to do; and the professional patient.

From a prognostic point of view we find that the professional patient is frequently the worst. He is articulate, cooperative, well-versed in the topic of his pathology, and highly alert to nuances in the therapist. He brings into the session all the qualities of an accessible subject. In brief, he is truly a professional. Since his skill is a product of years of training he will in most cases have run through a number of therapists.

Like the professional soldier, this patient has found a home. He does not come in order to change, but in order to perpetuate his particular kind of dependent relationship. When the therapist commences to reduce the expected support, the professional patient is apt to look for the next source of "theraperma." Worst perhaps of all, he usually leaves while still in tenacious ignorance of the game he is playing.

He is a product of the limitations of psychotherapeutic methods. The therapeutic effort remains confined to the time of the session which he attends in the manner of obtaining something like a periodic Viennese massage. The example of the professional patient throws focus on the need for something we will call patient's homework.

HOMEWORK

Traditionally, the beginning patient is admonished to go about his business as usual and to make no special allowances for the fact that he has now entered therapy. We have no quarrel with the intent of that advice, but we would warn about some of the uses to which the patient will put it.

The admonition to continue as usual, either explicitly given or tacitly assumed, can play directly into the hands of the attitude the professional patient has mastered so well: therapy, like church attendance, takes a set time per week, and as for the rest of the time, the devil take the hindmost, and never the twain shall meet. This is the reason why we suggest a regime which carries therapeutic effort and therapeutic techniques over and into the time which the patient does not spend with his therapist.

In the context of introducing the patient to the fact that therapy equals a special kind of hard work, we find it helpful to tell him that there will be homework right from the start. The comparison of the patient's overall life as the macrocosm and the sharply focused events of his session as a microcosm may aid in visualizing the essential identity of the two exposures. Do not forget that a vast number of patients enter psychotherapy the way they go to the dentist. The patient expects a certain amount of discomfort, he will hold very still for it, he will submit to expert ministrations which he himself cannot possibly perform. And the most lovable dentist is of course the most painless one.

Imagine, if you will, the dentist who sends his patient home to practice extractions and advises that you spend some diligent time every day in probing for nerves. Naturally, the knowing patient, the professional, is going to bolt that scene first. Though he will not be the only one. What we suggest by way of homework is almost that bad, but not quite.

While specific homework "prescriptions" will evolve throughout the course of therapy the general admonition is this: Once a day, in a quiet place where there will be no interruptions, spend a period of continuous time attending to the way you feel. The patient will learn the details later.

He can start with one minute at a time. The specific technique includes the following: Let your awareness range over your entire body. Focus on the part which calls attention to itself. If it is an itch or such like sensation, do not scratch it away. Stay with it. Allow "it" to show you what will happen next. Conversely, the focus may fall upon a "hole" in the body image, on an area of deadness. Stay with it. Bear the uncertainty of what will evolve next.

These are some of the simple exercises in attention paying, in self-awareness. We will describe them later as focusing techniques. They will demonstrate clearly how the patient is determined to interfere with himself, how anxiety leaps up at moments of uncertainty, how a block feels like thick cotton or solid wood.

It is apparent that the patient is asked to do for one minute a day (more later) what will undoubtedly be part of the therapeutic technique during a session.

The purpose of this basic homework is always to lead the patient to his areas of desensitization. Asked to attend to his feelings, and to his feeling-tone, he will also discover that he tends to switch with surprising frequency from attending to feeling to evolving fantasy. The distinction is of considerable technical importance—like the difference between what is and what might be—and puts the therapeutic effort during sessions that much further ahead.

As an adjunct to work in the sessions a homework prescription can have a specific purpose. The compulsive patient is asked to leave one part of his room or his table top in the very disorder which he thinks he cannot bear. For the bearable time which the patient can manage in homework he is asked to attend to his reaction to the mess, to the way it feels, what "it" wants him to do, or—in addition—to the evolving fantasy that might embellish and illuminate the state to which he is now attending.

Homework is most emphatically not to be construed as a project. Any routinization is death to the novel unfolding which is the purpose of homework. The free time which the patient is to find for himself every day for this work is less a daily routine than an interruption of routines in the rest of his day. This minute, this moment even, is the free time, the wild time if you will, during which the assumption of safety through control is slowly replaced by some leeway toward curiosity for the unexpected, where the numb senses reach out again for a wider spectrum.

Such unfolding is truly not a matter to be confined to the session. It is most certainly the very stuff of the confrontive experience. It is simply one more way toward expanding self-awareness.

The inclusion of homework in therapeutic work will impress the patient that his new effort is not confined to one hour a week and it will clearly show him that he is the responsible one in the process of cure. Not the least of advantages is the fact that this method will never allow for the making of a professional patient. In fact, we feel that it will help in the making of a person who is no patient at all.

chapter 3

The Growing Encounter

THE GAIN AND THE DANGER OF TRUST

Threat keeps the neurotic intact. His entire structure is designed to move from vulnerability to insensitivity. But now, as the patient moves into the therapeutic relationship, he does so because he is more willing to expose himself. As soon as he opens himself, allows himself to be touched, he becomes truly vulnerable. He is not yet hurt, but he leaves himself open to hurt. This risk is possible for him when he can trust.

Trust is simply the willingness to expose oneself without guarantees of absolute safety. Clearly, to develop trust in his therapist is no small endeavor for the patient, but without this sense of trust—this commitment to chance—therapeutic success cannot be achieved.

We are assuming, of course, that the therapist is indeed trustworthy in the relationship with his patient, that his actions do not stem from an intent to hurt. Trust is not given because the therapist wants it so, but because it is merited. There is no scrutiny quite like the neurotic's. He will test and retest the therapist's trustworthiness before he can allow himself to place even some of himself into jeopardy.

There is no point in urging the patient to place trust in the therapist. It would be as useless as legislating invulnerability. But we can help him to move toward trust (and eventually toward the knowledge that he can survive pain) by helping him to discover not what he lacks but what he has.

Instead of dealing with his absence of trust, we work with the presence of his distrust.

In the abstract, the man who is afraid to commit himself lacks trust. But in the concrete, he is actively engaged in a very live pursuit of distrusting himself and others. And if he did not, what would happen? He fears that he would be hurt again.

The next question is so general that it will apply almost anytime: What here threatens with harm?

The cues that are most concrete are the best. What, here-and-now, forbodes danger? The glint in the therapist's eye? His pasty hands? That tic in one nostril? His insufferable kindness? Whatever it is, the patient will eventually tell you.

The concern with this present situation which is essentially harmless will invariably lead the patient to the psychic wound which has remained to demand a life-style of distrust. The patient may have been genuinely mistreated in a past relationship, but at any rate a hurt has been sustained and the wound has not healed.

The clear and present response to a hurt is to hurt back, to damage the aggressor. If that intent is not expressed, the wound remains, the healing stays unfinished. If the situation of hurt can in no way be consummated with an expression of contingent anger, then anger cools into its own, icy shadow—hostility. When the focus of this present hostility falls on an object which is chronologically in the past, we then speak of resentment.

We reopen the patient's psychic wound. We find the focus of his hostility. And he knows what he resents. This moment of reentering what he considered a best-forgotten past will once again reopen him to present suffering. If, through the therapeutic work, he can now finish the unfinished situation, the wound can heal, and resentment has lost its function. The state that takes resentment's place has a warm aura of safe openness: it is forgiving.

The aspect of the person that can forgive can trust again, and the capacity that has been allowed to engender trust and forgiveness is love.

We have here described a therapeutic transformation which may typically occur quite early in the course of therapy. The patient has made concrete gains—and what does he see?

The evidence of gain is quite substantial: He has learned something new about himself and finished with one problem area. He has found trust again, he has learned that he can find rapport and grow through contact. He has, in the doing of this, commenced a journey from his periphery toward his center, and in the course of these events he has now also learned that his problems may well involve others, but that the barriers to his unfolding lie in himself.

He has weathered an instance of risk in discovery. He feels well. And now, why jeopardize success by going on to risk failure?

This is a critical juncture in the course of therapy. The patient, with the span of early sessions, finds the capacity to choose whether to stay or quit.

THE TERMINATION PROBLEM

The therapeutic exploration, even in early stages, may well deal with the most central problems of the patient's difficulties in his life encounter, but in the name of his sense of safety he has executed no more than a few skimming dives. He has now seen enough to realize that if he goes on, the risk goes on, if he delves deeper, the risk becomes greater.

We want to stress emphatically that early termination in and of itself does not mean that the patient is making a mistake.

The therapist may know that there are problem areas in the patient which can benefit from further work. In that sense, the termination may be premature. The patient may feel satisfied with his new level of awareness and decide that with this gain he wants to leave. The choice that counts is his.

Early terminations are not necessarily a flight, or a step designed to bring about a neurotic retrenchment. There is nothing specifically neurotic about quitting. The understanding gained feels satisfactory, there is no motivation to examine more. For that matter, brief therapy may be indicated from the start. The problem is specific, the patient has a good, regenerating core. Or termination may already be in order because the patient simply functions well enough again to operate in his own, chosen milieu.

A young woman twenty-three came for therapy because of increasingly frequent anxiety states. During the very early, supportive phase of her sessions she moved out of her parental home and joined a rural commune. Whether her ability to extricate herself from the pressures of her parent's home was in part a function of therapy remains a moot point. Before any such determination could become clear the young woman left therapy on her own decision. In the context of the commune, by the side of her devoted lover, and in a group of like-minded peers she functioned well at her assigned farming tasks, she became a freer person in her social contacts, and she developed new curiosities about a number of topics and subjects which she would not have dreamed of tackling before. In the context of her chosen milieu this young patient no longer needed therapy.

But then again the therapist may be confronted with the Problem Termination.

It occurs when the patient's gains are still supported by the therapeutic setting. Once the patient leaves, he will perforce of necessity fall back upon his neurotic style of meeting the crises of his life.

A physician, forty-five, came into therapy with the presenting complaint of a growing drug dependence. He had begun with occasional stimulants in order to be able to perform his work with a minimum of sleep. Next he began to balance the artificial excitation with suppressants, so that he could go to sleep at the instant when he felt that he could afford sleep. This regime of alternating sleeping pills and amphetamines, common enough today in some circles, did not strike the patient as a problem until he went on a month's vacation "in order to relax." He relaxed into a nervous collapse, so-called, with screaming insomnia on one hand and torpid and tremulous waking on the other. This state of ill-health emerged under absence of medication.

His own attempt at cure was "the therapy of work," as he chose to call it. He reentered his practice after two weeks of the relaxation which had been described, and naturally resumed his pill-taking again. He discovered, after his two weeks of quasi-abstinence, that his required dosage had doubled. At this point he entered psychotherapy.

Before any significant inroads were made into this patient's complementary problems of high, harsh standards of excellence on one hand and his established style of wheedling dependence on the other, he managed to reduce his drug dependence in an ingenious way: he reduced his workload radically, an unheard of step in his career, which he now justified by the explanation that he needed the time for psychotherapy. He reduced his punitive standards of achievement by increasing his dependence characteristics in his approach to psychotherapy.

Before this seesaw maneuver could come under effective scrutiny the patient left. He left ostensibly because he was now taking only an occasional sleeping pill, ditto amphetamines—"No more than I would prescribe for my own patients--." Diagonostically speaking, the imminent necessity to engage with his dependent style has caused him to terminate.

He was back shortly. Without the supportive use to which he had put the psychotherapeutic situation he had quickly reverted to the habitual behavior groove which had brought him into therapy in the first place. In this instance, the decision to terminate was almost entirely a matter of playing it safe, and this safety was sought within the shrinking confines of the patient's neurosis.

At such a point the therapist cannot be anything less than expert. He wants to show the patient that it is better to stay. He knows all the good reasons—and so does the patient, which is precisely why he wants to leave.

The therapist's expertness concerns the task of dealing with a person who teeters on an edge as never before. Expertness concerns the therapist's knowledge of just where the patient stands, how he stands, and when he might be falling. Good technique in therapy always involves a keen sensitivity to precisely the point of development at which the patient finds himself at the moment—but never is the demand as critical as when approaching a problem termination.

We look at the patient's level of self-esteem. Are you suggesting too much, and will he take it as a slur on his own ability?

We look at the patient's degree of self-support. Are you supplying too little, and is he reacting to the lack with the harsh conviction that you really don't care?

We look at the patient's ability to muster strength, plain and simple.

Are you going to wither it with mollifications or are you going to crush it with the threat of impossible problems?

To say the least, the entire therapeutic endeavor is in jeopardy.

Avoid spectacular maneuvers for getting at the patient. Interpretations, for example, can easily frighten him for good or they may simply render him dull. Reflective techniques contain the seed of personal indifference for the patient. Confrontations must be carefully gauged so that the patient knows you are with him, not against him.

In the service of a highly special circumstance—the problem termination—all these considerations of technique must be quite frankly juggled, where the switch from one approach to another is entirely determined by the chance that the patient may take flight in an instant.

He is in a state of wildly vacillating fright. Perhaps panic is imminent, but there is no perhaps about the fact that he can at an instant resort to the near and still dear armoring of his neurosis. It is his most readily available support, and it is precisely this support that is under fire.

The therapist's expertness, we have mentioned, lies in his sensitivity. It is the paramount quality here in demand. Unfortunately, this exercise of expertness is so complicated, and so alive, that it defies formulation as a simple rule. However, we have a simple rule—a far cry from being a substitute for the former—and that is the admonition to give the patient time.

At this point he needs time. He needs absence of demand, absence of pressure. He needs all this elbow-room to make his choice in freedom, while the therapist is there to help him.

Aside from the patient's statement that he might want to quit, the onset of a problem termination has characteristic signs: the patient falls back upon all his prevailing defenses against anxiety.

He becomes elusive. He discusses material that is largely irrelevant. He will confuse the therapist. When this begins to happen, we suggest that the patient be allowed to go on with his tricks. He knows he is on the brink of making an important decision and his maneuver is one of delay. By our rule of thumb, let him. Give him the time. The rule implies no amount of temporary indifference to the patient's workings. Do not deemphasize, for example, the brinkmanship of his condition. Talk about it. Do not belittle in fact or by default that he is here concerned with important life business. Loss of sensitivity to the patient's quest at this point—if only for one moment—can mean wasted work and a premature termination.

The therapist can make mistakes. He can damage the patient's self-esteem, for example. When that happens it is *de rigueur* to acknowledge the mistake and to make an apology. To say "I am sorry" can go a long way in teaching something about forgiveness. By and large, we have learned, the patient will accept soon enough that he is working with a fallible human being, and no damage done. But we are not talking now about by and large, we are talking about the crisis of a problem termination. In this case, please do *not* make any mistakes.

And then, hopefully, we look for the telltale signs that can show us that the patient wants to stay in therapy, or at any rate, that he is giving it serious thought.

His old servants and all his old keepers desert him. He suffers a breakdown of characterological defenses. His report will be puzzled and anxious: old obsessional ruminations, old phobic avoidances, the gamut of his customary repressive mechanisms, they no longer work! Characteristically, there may occur a marked increase in the patient's anxiety at this turning point in early therapy.

He gives another indication of his tentative choice. The patient becomes coercive. This attempt to direct the therapist is in most instances a resistance maneuver, an attempt to avoid confrontation. But in the context of the problem termination, the clear meaning is also that he is not taking off, but that—on his terms—he means to stay. Please note here that the patient, among other things, is undoubtedly engaged in a trial act and, as with all trial acts, when something new is attempted the result may well be a grotesque exaggeration. It is very important for the therapist not to interpret unreasonable assertiveness as a shotgun attack upon his own existence. It may be target practice, but it is not assault with intent to kill. It may be the first muscle the patient is showing, now that he has decided that he will engage.

WHO IS THE BOSS?

Nobody.

Nevertheless, the problem raised by the question is not a straw man. Both patient and therapist will encounter their own problem of wanting to put down the other, or to raise him unnaturally.

The therapist, unsure of himself or his skill, may to varying degrees feel victimized by a patient's coercive efforts. In regard to the patient's behavior we would like to distinguish between the assertiveness which is a trial act, as mentioned above, and a truly coercive act which is part and parcel of the patient's character. This style is based on the abiding need to overpower the other one, an attitude which belongs to the "spoiled-brat syndrome," as described by Alfred Adler. In that case, a person is willing to wreck anything in order to attain immediate satisfaction for some tyrannical need.

If this form of coercion is encountered, the point of therapeutic contact is not the patient's power need per se. Instead, let the focus fall on the existential experience of being a spoiled brat. It is difficult to outmaneuver such a patient with a reverse power play as an answer. Most important, it is therapeutically useless. The therapist may get his temporary kick from demonstrating superior strength and skill, but the patient will either feel injured or he will get much trickier. Instead of getting sucked in by the patient's manipulations, it is essential to stay with the power play phenomenon itself as the object of therapeutic work.

The therapist with doubts of self-worth may slide into subtle manipulations of his own, such as guiding the patient toward praising the therapist and extolling the wonders of the therapeutic progress. Once again this is not therapy, because now one partner exists only in terms of the needs of the other.

The beginning therapist needs supervision to spot the sliding play of who does what to whom and who comes out on top. If this is not enough to keep the therapist free from the patient's manipulations and to keep the therapist's own psychological problems from hindering the patient, then personal psychotherapy is a must. Otherwise, only the most superficial patient difficulties can be handled by the therapist and even on that level his professional skills can be unpredictably misused.

Status problems about who is allowed to do what to whom are different in the case of the patient in one instance only.

Our entire social climate is apt to breed the assumption that when you go to someone for help you submit to the expert's superior skills. The patient would be particularly sensitive to this expectation because of his ready association between psychotherapy and medicine.

The traditional relationship between doctor and patient is one of almost total dependence. The sufferer comes to the healer who alone has the secret knowledge which is required to effect a cure. The patient comes in order to have something done to him. The doctor tells him what is wrong and what to do. And then he makes the patient well. The patient submits and the doctor cures.

Psychotherapists know that this is not the nature of the psychotherapeutic relationship, that instead only the active participation of both can get results. This entire book deals with this thesis. Our point is that the patient may not be aware of it.

Sometimes a brief explanation on the topic is enough to start the patient's reorientation. Sometimes it might in effect be the subject matter of status in the relationship that will come up, if any one-way relationship of superior-inferior, of leader-follower, is allowed to maintain itself, there is something wrong—with the therapist.

The therapeutic relationship is not an equal one in the sense of what each partner needs, but it is equal in the requirement that each must give all he can. That consideration has obviously nothing to do with status, a concept that has no place in the therapeutic relationship. Status is established on the basis of judgments which evaluate how much of a desirable thing one man has as compared to another. No matter what the desirable attribute may be, any status evaluation must depend on the qualities of the other one.

From our existential point of view this is a waste of time, talent, and the truth of what I am. We are dependent on each other in various ways, but a person's capacity for any fulfillment rests only with him. Psychotherapy helps with that.

ON LYING TO THE PATIENT

We mention lying only because intentional misinformation has sometimes been used for reasons of helpfulness. We are concerned with lying because it has an effect on the liar, on the listener, and on the relationship of the two people involved. This is the extent of our "moral" concern. Any other concern, such as matters of principle in this area, is redundant. With abstractions as our beacon the issue soon drifts away from the moorings of the existential event, so that an insistence on abstract truthfulness, for example, may assume bizarre proportions. Consider the therapist who in the name of truth will tell all. He will tell how he feels, how he reacts, what he sees, or what preoccupies him. Note, if you will, that all this openness is developed in the name of a principle. But what of the existential event, in this case the therapeutic situation?

As for the therapist: he expresses himself. As for the patient: he is being swamped. As for the therapeutic relationship: it becomes something between muddled and none.

The therapist has used the patient for his own purposes, regardless of the patient's particular existential situation at that moment. Guided by principles, the therapist has lost touch.

Conversely, a brief note on the intentional misstatement, the lie. Its commitment has one instant consequence. It splits the liar in two-; I who knows and the I who says are no longer the same.

A lie does not reflect the existential event which it purports to describe. That is the purpose of the lie, and its poison. The effect of this purposeful split into appearance and reality is the consequential destruction of direct communication. Contact is poisoned or lost. Instead of contact, a distance has been made. Note, for example, how the purpose of this contact break functions in three different situations. Lying to a stranger tends to be a complete matter of indifference as far as the effective relationship between the liar and the victim is concerned. A contact situation is not at issue between strangers. But lying to an enemy may be a victorious pleasure. The separation effect, the deception, is precisely the intended consequence of hostile contact. And for the final situation, to show the effect of the lie: When a lie passes between lovers, the created split and distance is a sad and a very destructive event.

The protective purpose of the neurosis depends on the lie. There is the distance of impersonality in contact with another—the effect of the self-split in the act of the lie. There is the assaultive trickery of the neurotic who poisons every relationship with the deception he has chosen as a guard against enemies from within and without. The more available the lie is to the neurotic, the more comfortable he feels. The person who is abandoning his neurosis lies only with difficulty and with a sense of discomfort.

Deception is the shield of neurosis. Keep in mind that the patient will be a past master at this. He will know the signs when the therapist uses deceit.

Clearly then, the pathogenic nature of lying runs precisely counter to the therapeutic endeavor. The therapist who lies serves no therapeutic purpose. Instead, he leaves the existential scene, he loses touch both with himself and the patient, and he introduces the distance which he is trying to break down.

But the issue of lying actually comes up only because the patient will often ask a question that the therapist does not want to answer.

There is the time-honored dodge of the professional who then says: "Can you tell me a little bit more about that?"

What he means is: "I wish you'd say less." Now he has lied.

Instead, the therapist stays with himself, and with his patient, when he answers the unwanted question without trickiness: "I don't want to tell you right now."

Neither patient nor therapist can now drift off into shadow-boxing or into deceptive games of hide-and-seek. At this game the patient, once again, is a past master, or else therapy would not take so long. And he is in therapy not to perpetuate that situation, but to find a new way.

We do not hold with the moldy apologia that the end justifies the means. On the contrary, the way that is taken may demean the end. Indeed, the way is the end.

THE BEGINNING OF DIRECT CONFRONTATION

Until now, therapy was mostly a meeting of strangers who are learning to know each other. The therapist has tried to feel the patient out and the patient has fenced with the therapist. Then a manner of trust has developed. The therapist has stopped groping. He sees more clearly. The patient has stopped parrying each move. He feels safer. At this juncture the therapist can begin to use confrontation.

When he acts from his center he can confront without fear of hurting the patient. At center there is no corrective judgment, no punitive criticism, no repartee for the sake of besting the other. If the foreground phenomenon in the session is the patient's fear and hesitation, the therapist can say: "You look afraid."

From the center, this is a reflection of fact, an expression of compassion. But the tone, the look, all the cues that convey intent could come out quite differently if the remark came from the therapist's need to belittle the patient or to imply his own savage fearlessness. That comment would, in our vocabulary, come from the periphery. It can injure the patient. The act from the center does not harm.

When responding from his center, the therapist is free to respond directly and always remain therapeutic. This freedom to respond without blocks and without premeditation will enhance the patient's growth immeasurably. The patient is truly allowed to affect another human being who does not resort to all the manipulative and the defensive tricks of the periphery. This allows for close touch. The experience may be an eyeopener for the patient simply in terms of witnessing a new form of behavior; for here is someone who can be open and warm without fear of destruction, without need for defense. The example is not curative, but it may give a glimpse of an entirely new horizon.

As long as the masks remain on, as long as the partners still use their pretended, their assumed exteriors for mutual presentation, for all that time they will waltz about in the arms of their respective illusions. And they will hardly ever meet.

The one in the sackcloth and ashes plays the role of a patient, and the one with the bland mien and the earnest eye enacts the therapist. The masked ball is endless and gets duller with time ... until somebody stops pretending and shows the living face—no matter how pale by now—which the mask has crowded out.

In confrontation the mask slips, drops, and may be discarded. There is no point in trying to predict what will show now. The patient who begins to open under confrontation will be varied, capricious, new, unexpected, and no longer so intent on continuing his repetitious waltz. The therapist, without programmed responses, will have to draw mainly on his own spontaneity. It comes from his center. When he is at center his range of responses and his tolerance for experience will indeed be wide. His capacity to respond and his tolerance for experience are of course precisely what makes it possible for him to be a therapist.

There is a manner of guide for the direction of his responses. The therapist proceeds according to his knowledge of the patient's needs and at a pace which the patient can bear at the time. The direction of therapy at this point is the confrontation with illusion. The intent is the dissolving of illusion.

Repeatedly the therapist can now confront the patient with parts of his desensitized areas. These are the parts of the personality which the patient has masked and has kept out of awareness.

"I see sharpness in your mouth. Can you feel it? I hear the sharpness in your voice. Did you hear it? Shall I say it the way you did? You showed me your resentment."

During these beginning attempts to confront the patient with aspects of his personality which, so far have remained hidden, the patient responds increasingly with the wide-eyed feeling of being misunderstood.

Significantly, the patient's reaction is not one of instant denial or disagreement. Instead, there is at least a touch of genuine surprise.

We are not suggesting that the patient will then turn with wonder and look at the awesome quality of himself which the therapist has been trying to bring into view for him. The scotoma remains, and it is of course the doctor who does not see this thing right.

The old patterns of behavior—like old soldiers—die hard. Patients will hang on to long-established aspects of their behavior even after they see that their habitual ways of responding no longer work for them. In a figurative sense, it almost seems as if these subconstellations of their make-up have a life of their own—and that they mean to preserve it.

Any living organism will oppose its own dissolution and the habitual patterns of behavior which have for so long maintained themselves (without integration into the rest of the organism) which have come to act automatically in defense of themselves; they are truly like autonomous entities.

"I don't want to turn nasty, but then it just happens, whenever you set me off!"

When this *it* has again become I, when the patient again feels that he is responsible for turning on or turning off, then the next step toward wholeness has been taken.

But while the autonomy of the subpattern is intact there is a row to hoe. As the therapist continues to come back to the desensitization the patient will resort to blocks. In this context, the block most frequently takes the form of such astounding denseness that the therapist's patience may be put to a brutal test. This mulishness of not seeing, of not moving, is purely defensive. It is a good point to remember when at the limits of patience.

A part of the patient does not want to die. The block which takes the form of moronic stupidity is of course no reflection on the patient's intelligence nor—and this is much more important—does it reflect dullness in the rest of the make-up. This blockish, stultified patient is aware of every nuance of change in the therapist, particularly when there is a move from the center to the periphery when impatience, anger, or when loss of interest might occur. Then the therapist loses the patient. The block has worked.

The ability of the patient to misunderstand can take a less massive, a much more fanciful form when the active defense slides to the verbal level. Many patients are verbally agile to begin with and have sharpened their endowment over years of maintaining their neurosis intact. They will paraphrase the therapist's observation and thereby side-step its point. If this goes on long enough and is done nimbly enough, the therapist might suddenly find himself explaining the ultimate nature of what he really meant.

One explanation demands another and now therapy has metamorphosed into an argument. Both partners are performing a circular dance around the totem pole of concept upon concept.

The defense has worked. Instead, stay with the phenomenological fact that the patient, here and now, is engaged in defending. When the therapist continues to point to the stance, the act, the event of the defending maneuvers, the patient may not be able to escape the experience of what he is doing, instead of drowning awareness with the flood of his talk. When he has made contact with this denied aspect of himself, once again he has added to his wholeness.

We have saved the real disaster for last: The therapist *does* misunderstand the patient.

At this juncture an apology might help as much as a cough drop helps with tuberculosis.

A critical point had been reached when trust developed between patient and therapist. Now, as confrontation begins, this trust receives its test.

A mistake in either seeing or understanding the patient is likely to be taken by the patient as proof of his own correctness in seeing things. He has allowed himself to look in a new way, a painful way, and he sees nothing new. Then why do it? And if the patient is vindictively inclined he may alter his image of the therapist beyond recognition.

In brief, once again—no mistakes at this point, please.

The more the therapist can view from the center the less he distorts what comes his way. There are various moments at which the therapist makes conclusions, but there is no time when he does not observe. He wants to see what is there, because he truly does not know ahead of time. He wants to know how it all hangs together, because any patient's structuring is at best only partly similar to something the therapist has seen before. When the therapist has recognized what he sees and is ready to help the patient in confrontation, then it is best to engage with the patient on an almost entirely phenomenological level. Explanations are an attempt to see for the patient. Abstract discussion is an interpretive change. The closer both observation and discourse stick to the phenomenological level, the less chance is there for error and the more chance for the patient's clear view.

EXISTENTIAL ANXIETY: CRISIS IN ACTION

The dialogue of confrontation does not often occur socially. This dialogue demands answers from the depths of the participants and this demand touches the existing limits of the personality. In this way the hidden, the hoarded, the guarded, and the forbidden, any or all of these aspects of the participants' make-up may be called into play. Therefore, confrontation in therapy will bring forth anxiety.

This is not the so-called neurotic anxiety which might have been part and parcel of the patient's behavioral mode. This new anxiety is neither triggered by phobic objects, nor does it arise out of established conditioning. This is not the revival of an historic event. Instead, it is a direct result of the psychotherapeutic encounter. It is the birth of a trauma, not its mummified remains. Therapist and patient are witness to the crisis *in situ*.

The patient who is a novice may save himself from the ongoing event by some ready explanation. He has always felt this nervous, he might say, when he forgets to sit up straight and instead slouches in his seat, which puts pressure on his belly. The seasoned patient may lift the unmanageable reality of the emerging anxiety to a level of manageable abstractions. He knows, so runs the explanation, that this sort of vis-à-vis with the therapist is symbolic of constipation caused by confinement to the chamber pot at age two.

But what is happening?

This discomfort is happening, and this lame explanation, and this threat of anxiety—is happening.

In our view the outcome of psychotherapy is affected more instrumentally by paying attention to the ongoing experience than by any exploratory technique which tends to depart from the encountered event of the moment.

For example, the therapist observes that the patient is behaving like a spoiled child. At one level of analysis this behavior may well reflect the patient's habitual conduct with an aggressive, dominating father, but so far as the available evidence for the diagnosis is concerned, the interpretation is no more than an educated guess. However, what exists experientially, in contrast to theoretically, is the present feeling in the present situation with the therapist. In our view, this encounter experience is the beginning—and sometimes the end—of any therapeutic endeavor. We therefore suggest that the therapist do not commence his work with a diagnostic guess but with the phenomenon which he faces: The patient behaves like a spoiled child. The observation now becomes a response: "I see you behaving like a spoiled child."

In this example the patient now feels misunderstood, or insulted, or rejected, the assumption of a safe relationship with the therapist is immediately in doubt. While in doubt about the safety of his condition, while the patient commits no resolving act, he hangs in existential anxiety.

The moment of risk has arrived. Here is the chance of losing the therapist's good will, his affection, and his continued understanding.

More often than not the patient will prefer to suffer the silent anguish of holding still rather than take the demonstrable risk of reacting to the therpist while there is no guarantee that the best of all possible reactions will be produced. This moment of risk may immobilize the patient, but it better not immobilize the therapist. It is his responsibility to respond to the patient's dominant state—his existential anxiety—and to enter the encounter before its substance goes dead. He responds: "I have made you angry."

Perhaps this is not true and the patient's subsequent reactions will tell a better tale, but at the very least the very best has been achieved: The immediacy of the encounter has been maintained. If there was anger, it has not been allowed to hide without recognition. If there was anxiety without the definitive content which lets the patient recognize just what he is feeling, then the vagueness of focus becomes the proper content of what is now known to exist.

There is no comfort of stasis in ongoing therapy. In the flux of the confrontive encounter there is only the comfort of changing a suspended state into an act of completion. Until this move toward completion occurs, there is anxiety.

The very frequency of this anxiety may be the barometer of the pressure for movement which must be there, if motion is to occur. When the patient moves, when the suspension of an act becomes an act being committed, then anxiety becomes excitement. The word *excitement* describes the psychological state in which energy, freed for use, is now being used.

In brief, successful confrontation progresses from stasis, to anxiety, to excitement, and so to an act of change.

Our emphasis at this point is on the meaning of anxiety. It means that growth movement is not yet; and it means that stasis is no more. Psychological stasis contains no potential for growth, but anxiety does. Anxiety, the state when rigid control fails homeostatically, becomes the necessary condition for renewed psychological function.

The thawing of a frostbitten hand is accompanied by pain. The hand may not work for a time, but instead of ending in death it has come back to life.

Anxiety is the halfway house on the road of growing. We feel that any psychological change that contains no evidence of anxiety does not lead toward growth.

This statement is a work criterion when observing the patient who changes under the stress of the confrontive encounter.

Here is a patient whose symptoms vanish. His constrictive self-rule disappears. There is a clear, sometimes dramatic shift in the patient. And all these observable alterations in the patient's approach to the therapist occur with smooth aplomb and without anxiety. This is the flight into health.

Improvement without the signs of anxiety is an evasive maneuver by the patient under confrontive stress.

The message is as naïve as it is clear: "Look! No need to go on with all this unpleasantness, and the flattery of 'Well done!' to my Instant Therapist!"

The patient may remain completely unaware of the nature and intent of his shift. Without need for conscious participation an autonomous set of conditioned reactions take over as the status quo comes under attack. The patient has defended his neurotic integrity and he has diminished the chance of further confrontive assaults—that is, if the therapist too remains unaware of the nature of the shift.

The signs of this critical evasion on the part of the patient are improvements that occur soon, suddenly, and painlessly.

The actual maneuver will vary with the patient's resources. There may be great cleverness in duplicating the behavioral change which the therapist would like to see. We will paraphrase a patient's maneuver which illustrates both the naïveté of the switch and the cleverness with which it was introduced. This patient, a woman of forty-two who had no problem with verbal expressiveness, turned protectively monosyllabic as confrontation zeroed insistently on the patient's symptom of sudden sweats. Hour after hour, so it seemed to the patient, the hard-working therapist tried to encourage talk. "This indefatigable prober for the soft spot," thought the patient, "has one obvious complaint which gives him—and me—no rest. He wants me to talk. Well then, let there be talk."

And now the patient talked. The confronting topic was the sudden sweat which the patient had experienced on her way to the session. She had stopped her car at the red light. When the red switched to green she felt "the skin turn into a sponge, like glutted with moisture, and then a great pressure, like a squeeze from the inside. I was drenched. Like a flood coming out of me."

The abbreviated tape of the exchange at this point contained this maneuver:

Patient: I was not in any great discomfort, really, but was perfectly willing to contemplate this.

Therapist: Can you do it now?

Patient: Of course. As I continued down the street I stopped sweating but actually still felt this skin feeling I just described to you but there was a breeze on it now. There was the nicest breeze now which I could see in the trees along the street. I love the feel of it on my skin, and in my hair, which is a lot like those treetops waving around in it, don't you think?"

Therapist: I think you lost me.

Patient: Why don't you listen?

Therapist: I listen and I hear you getting me into the trees.

Patient: I haven't come to the important thing yet. You see, there is something very sensuous about the wind, wind feeling its way through trees and all that. Sexual, really. To me, you understand, the nature of the sexual is a mingling—I am thinking of tree foliage and wind—and I told you about that friend of my girl friend's and me that time we were kids—well, not really kids—you remember that incident that was so—that sexual summer I told you about?"

Therapist: I remember.

With a rather naive trickiness the topic was changed from the sweat experience to something of deep, dirty significance. The therapist should love this. The talk turns to sex. But the captivating content of the topic notwithstanding, the therapeutic focus of the therapist must remain on the phenomenal event of his encounter with the patient. What is going on? The patient has switched topics. She related a skin experience during a particular event and then turned to a metaphoric discourse on sexual mingling which she topped off with a footnote about an afternoon of intercourse. She had related the incident before. She did not reexperience it now but simply referred to it for the benefit of the therapist's fantasy life. After the brief reference to the sweat experience she had turned facile in manner and delivery and instead of feeling the content of her descriptions through she became discursive and quite entertaining in manner.

Was there concern, anxiety, interest, involvement with content, or was there involvement with delivery? In brief, *what* was the patient doing?

The question is relevant because the therapist must stay with the patient, not with the patient's verbiage, or else he is responding to someone who is not really there. The shift in the patient is designed precisely to engage the therapist with someone who is not really there. The patient who sweats and does not want to know about that experience, she is there. She is the one who is now waving about a distracting lure.

Perhaps the therapist sees that the shift has occurred, or perhaps he is simply confused by what seems like a leap in the topic.

"You lost me," is the honest, the contactful, the therapeutic response. "This is steamy stuff about you and those other two, but you left me at the red traffic light."

The therapist has given notice. He is not walking into a trap. If the shift was not a trap, he has stayed nevertheless with his phenomenological situation. He has in either event said, "Where am I?" which is rather frequently the only honest thing that he can say. And now the patient is no longer the manipulator of a trap, or if there was no trap, no longer a product of the therapist's own illusion. He is again, because of the confrontive response by the therapist, a participant.

Which is, of course, precisely what the patient in a shift did not want to be.

The patient can talk about a topic without having any present experience of its content. When the therapist focuses on the topical content alone, he leaves out the only subject matter of the moment, namely the patient and his ways of responding to the therapist.

Any topic can be relevant in the psychotherapeutic situation. Its relevance, however, is only discovered by its effect on the contact between patient and therapist.

Is the patient leaving you behind? Are you ahead of the patient? In either event, contact becomes tenuous. This may be due to the maneuvers of the patient or due to the therapist's lack of skill.

We know of only one way to regain contact that has been lost. It is not by going back to the former topic. It is not by going ahead to the next story. It is simply to know where you are now. The touchstone of learning where we are is always in the question: What have you and I done to this present situation?

The dialogue that roots the therapeutic encounter in the available present contains all the questions and responses which make known what each person is doing. When the patient talks topics, or when he is switching them, the guiding question remains: What is the patient doing with the content of his delivery? Then, once again, the focus of therapeutic attention remains on the proper study of the session, namely the man or woman who came for help.

chapter 4

Toil and Trouble: Techniques

The self that emerges at this stage of therapy is a delicate thing. The patient who divests himself of the constraints imposed by rigid patterns of behavior and who now dares for the first time to question his tried though untrue illusions also loses his sense of customary support. While he is largely committed to change at this point in therapy his judgment of what is safe and what is dangerous still scans therapeutic action like an unblinking eye. While he may well trust the therapist now; he just barely trusts himself.

"I know you won't let me drown," one patient said very much to the point, "but the fact is I don't swim so well."

So that our patient's unblinking eye might find some rest, we watch him from our center, and we try to take care. The accord which we have with him, our regard of impersonal empathy for him, may now well be achieved quickly as a session begins. This accord and this touch with one another is not a technique, but it is a state of tuning in on each other. The condition deserves a brief section.

TUNING IN ON EACH OTHER

There are characteristics entirely unique to the contact in the therapeutic encounter. For example, they are emphatically not those of a scientific inspection.

The object of attention is not an object but a process of interaction. The interaction has no objective controls but is only generated by subjective participation involving the whole person, in contrast to only the brain filtering an impression, an eye noting a shape, a pulse racing with compassion. Piecemeal presence and exclusive use of special faculties will not do. Contact is not achieved by any preset programming of a sending-receiving device. We are not interested in a record of events. A tape recorder, in that respect, is better than a therapist.

Therapy as such is a particular change—in exchange. Somehow, the awareness of the ongoing therapeutic event requires that the patient and the therapist become tuned in on each other.

How?

This is a risky section for us because it fairly demands some rendition of program notes. But since the last time we tuned in while in session, one of the authors claims to have forgotten the program and the other maintains that he would not use the same program again. A *post facto* attempt at program notes turned into a post-mortem and that, of course, deals with something dead. The session, however, was not.

How did we tune in? It was as if we walked into each other's house. Like good guests, we minded our manners. Nothing got broken. We did not dribble on the rug. We each brought a gift, though language fails us when we try to describe what it was. But we know distinctly that when we left each other, we each owned something new. This is what happened when we were in tune with each other. Because of this the session had been good. In fact, we and the patient looked forward to the next meeting, even though there was some notion that we would soon run into the following matter. . . .

THE RESISTANCES

Now the patient stops moving ahead. It is true that he seems to be of two minds on the matter—he has not stopped for a comfortable rest—but the impetus to move on and the mute force which holds him still are locked in a worrisome stasis.

There are a variety of meanings to the word *resistance*, but as a point of departure for us we would like to mention the psychoanalytic use of the term, which is perhaps the most specific. A resistance is the state that operates in the patient who finds himself unable to move in the direction suggested by the analyst. The patient cannot go ahead because he resists.

We give the term a slightly different emphasis because we want to stress the operations performed by the patient when he uses resistance.

Resistance is any condition in which the patient produces lack of feeling with the purpose of blocking or of interrupting effective expansion of his ongoing awareness.

In the context of this broad meaning the resistance described in psychoanalysis becomes a specific instance of "resistance in therapy." In contrast to the psychoanalytic emphasis, our slight alteration of describing resistance produces some operational advantages: any resistance is now an instance of desensitization, whether on the intellectual level (of not knowing), the physical level (of not sensing), or the emotional level (of not feeling).

There is purpose in desensitization: a resistance indicates intent to be unaware. But even without the teleology, the fact remains that the desensitized person exists now in a state of reduced exposure and operates removed from the pressure of particular psychological functions. Whatever has been interrupted by resistance will no longer enter awareness. It is prevented from expression, and it does not demand action.

Resistance functions to maintain the status quo. Desensitizations are antichange, whether the change is toward psychological expansion or toward psychological contraction.

The sensation of change is excitement. The sensation of stemming the flow of change is anxiety. And the haven of a well-functioning resistance is to feel nothing at all.

We have mentioned before that it is diagnostic of fakery when apparent change is not accompanied by anxiety. The partial flowing which is the commencement of change when a resistance dissolves must be felt—and this feeling is anxiety.

This sensation occurs typically whether the change from stasis toward movement is in the direction of growth (i.e., expansion), or in the direction of retrenchments within shrinking confines of safety. By the same token, a full commitment to change is marked by excitement whether the direction is growth or reduction. There is excitement in the patient who changes from fixed, moral judgments to boundless, amoral acceptance. Conversely, there is excitement in the patient who changes from a boundless sense of responsibility in a world of pain to a set of value patterns which always blame others for his pains.

In which direction the patient moves is entirely his business, and his choice. Of course, his showing up in therapy means that his choice no longer feels so good. His resistances work at less than perfection. He wants better ones, or fewer ones, or at any rate he does not want those that he has now.

But psychotherapy is not a shop for the repair of resistances. Psychotherapy works to make resistances flexible or to remove them entirely, and the therapeutic encounter is specifically designed to make all this a little more attainable. It makes choice possible.

Defense mechanisms, which we regard as specific instances of resistance, have been the subject of intensive analysis by Freudian therapists. Both Sigmund and his daughter Anna Freud have written at length on the subject, and where the patient presents the so-called classical neurotic difficulties—the very ones that served to develop psychoanalytic descriptions—there the analysis of defense mechanisms produces the desired results.

But the individual devises and develops resistance in a great variety and in ingenious ways. The patient may do this with no special regard for the classical form. Wilhelm Reich, for example, discovered that his analysis of defense mechanisms was severely impeded by the patient's use of psychomotor tensions. His necessary modification of Freud's method commenced to deal with the "recovery" of repressed impulses by treating psychomotor defenses as the symptoms which required analysis.

Very often this modification of classic psychoanalysis, viz., Reich's character analysis, is today more appropriate than straight Freudian psychoanalysis. The patient with classic neurotic symptoms seems on the wane. Instead he appears increasingly as a person whose character, in Fenichel's dramatic phrase, "is ripped and torn."

An impulse impels action and an act is performed through the motion of musculature. If an impulse must be curtailed or interrupted then the musculature will have to implement the curtailment of motion. And if the defense against the impulse becomes habitual then the somatic equivalent must be an habitual, characteristic way of bodily movement. For this reason we can speak of resistances implemented by the musculature. We feel that all resistances are located in the musculature.

A small child finds a newborn brother in the house. If the child discovers that the presence of the baby means less attention from the mother, then, in the absence of other compensations for the loss, the child may grow resentful of the baby whose presence has destroyed the child's stable comfort. The child now reacts with the impulse to destroy, and at one point the pressure of the impulse may be keen enough to precipitate an effective, muscular act. The child hits the baby.

The mother, witness to this simple act, protects the helpless baby with a strong "No" to the older child, with an angry slap, with a cold absence of affection.

Sooner or later the villainous child takes these consequences of his actions into account with the same simple logic that made him hit the baby in the first place. The next time he experiences the impulse to strike he interrupts the surge of his muscular tonus. The impulse is felt and is somatically interrupted. This willed and felt act is called *suppression.*

Its continued exercise may soon achieve better efficiency. There is a gradual change in the use of the musculature. The sensation of tonus interruption is no longer experienced. The impulse is no longer felt. There is now a demonstrable desensitization of the musculature and a lack of impulse awareness. The efficient child has achieved *repression.*

The child's repression may survive as the adult's elaborate habit. The aggressive impulse finds acceptable expression in the mannerism of clenching a fist or of stiffening a shoulder. The chronic control of the relevant musculature may produce bursitic conditions, breath suspension, guarded voice qualities, or some bodily evidence that is the opposite of an aggressive act. This hitter of babies now stands with a shy hunch to his shoulders and he looks about with a saccharine smile.

We are talking about the psychology of expressive behavior. All our musculature gives expression to the manner in which we have handled life experiences. Our posture, gate, articulation of movement, our talk, laugh, and tilt of the head all reflect in some way our habitual conflict solutions.

As existential psychotherapists we look for the phenomenon in the patient's musculature. We want to learn the patient's body language.

Except for our vocabulary, none of this may seem very different from the Freudian approach to behavior and psychotherapy. However, our description reflects our particular approach, and our approach differs very clearly in the manner of handling resistances. We engage them on a level which we find more accessible to therapeutic work than psychoanalytic exploration. We will look for the resistance complex.

This is not the search for classic defense mechanisms whose constellation is defined ahead of time. We look for *this* patient's unique web of entwined resistances, because this resistance complex makes up the patient's present mode of living and his particular way of being in this world.

We have described a point of view. We will now show how we use it.

HOW TO DEAL WITH RESISTANCES

We deal with resistances on the level at which they are known to the patient and in the form in which the patient can experience them. The resistance has a contemporary function. It has a present value for the patient. That is the focus of our therapeutic attention.

Behind every resistance lies unfinished business which the resistance encapsules and keeps from the patient's view. The resistance is successful to the extent that the patient feels no pain of knowledge or pang of curiosity about what he is hiding from himself. We work with those resistances that draw attention to themselves because they have begun to crack. It is their inefficiency of containing unfinished business that makes them call attention to themselves as an experience of discomfort.

A 38-year-old woman, divorced for ten years, came into therapy with a presenting complaint of anorexia. She was a highly successful business woman. Very much in keeping with her supervisory excellence in business, she not only came to the sessions with a complaint but also had a plan for the correct manner of treatment. Her loss of appetite, so went her diagnosis, was the consequence of the general self-denial which successful execution of her business duties demanded of her. Her aim: How to find pleasure without relaxation of duties. Her procedure: Learn how to make better use of time.

We asked her fairly early what the sensation of no appetite was like but she brushed the question aside as irrelevant. "Besides, I've looked into that," was her comment. "There is no sensation."

The resistance involved did not become accessible for some time. When it did, the crack in the sensory resistance took the following form. While making reference to a slight headache the patient kept working her hand over her throat.

Therapist: What are you doing with your hand?

Patient: Nothing.

Therapist: Now that you've taken your hand away, what does your throat feel like?

Patient: Uh, no particular feeling. It's the headache.

Her throat worked and then the patient coughed. During the subsequent silence the patient coughed again, then smiled in a forced fashion.

Patient: Just a dry throat. Incidentally, my headache is getting better.

Therapist: Please stay with your dry throat.

Patient: What is there to stay—say, I mean?

Therapist: I see you swallowing.

Patient: No, I was trying to. I was not swallowing. It's too dry, I told you.

Therapist: And? Please feel it through.

Patient: And, I'd say—

Therapist: What does the throat say?

Patient: How could it? It's clamping shut.

Since, in this instance, the therapist had the visual evidence of muscular work in the throat, he could continue with what he saw.

Therapist: I don't see that it's shut and done with it. I see movement.

Patient: Well, of course. It's trying to shut, is what I meant.

Therapist: What is the throat doing? Shutting out? Holding in?

The answer was not verbal. The patient began to salivate, very suddenly and excessively, and with an expression of utter anguish she then swallowed rapidly. When she relaxed and could speak again she reported that the sensation of disgust had been unmistakable.

The resistance had begun to give way and patient and therapist had their first glimpse of the unfinished business which desensitization in the mouth, nose, and throat, and rigidity in the esophageal musculature had kept hidden from her.

When a resistance gives way it is not a pleasant business. When a resistance clamps shut, the relief may by no means be total, just as utter silence after great noise may have the frightening sense of vacuity which comes with loss of touch. In either event, when the patient experiences a resistance, stay with him and give him support. Because he will now have to stay with an unpleasant experience.

This technical point is in distinct contrast to the techniques which favor interpretation. But we would like to avoid the difficulty of proper timing by which success of interpretation stands or falls. An interpretation is properly timed when the patient accepts it and makes the new knowledge his own. This cannot occur until he first knows that he is doing a number of things to prevent himself from knowing. The preventive agent *is* the resistance. He must know that first. That is why we stay with the resistance.

We do not ask *why* there is a resistance, the unfortunate question which instantly propels us beyond the experiential event and into speculation. We ask *how* does the resistance work, and *what* does it do. Here, from part of a tape, is an example.

The patient talks and then suddenly he falters and stops. Don't ask why he has stopped, a question which likely as not evokes a variety of spurious rationalizations and guesses. Instead: "What stops you?"

"It's like I've come up against a wall."

The question has concentrated the patient's attention on the experienced event. The responsive answer reflects what the patient actually feels. He feels stopped by a wall which is his experience of the resistance. Now stay with the resistance by staying with the patient's experience of the wall.

"What kind of a wall?"

"That's silly. I'm thinking of a hundred other things."

"We will try to learn what you know, not what you think. The wall is something you can really know. You just ran into it. Look at it."

"It's blank."

"Touch it."

"Okay—blank."

"It looks blank. How does it feel?"

"Blank is smooth. It feels smooth. God damn it, that wall has no give at all! Hard as steel!"

"What is it doing to you?"

"Well, obviously, it's keeping me out. I can't get to the other side."

"How does that make you feel?"

"I'm getting mad. I am really getting mad in some terribly helpless way."

"Nothing you can do."

"Now just a minute, I didn't say that. If I had a ladder, for example—"

"Doesn't sound so helpless anymore. Alright, let's get a ladder."

"You got a ladder?"

"Yes. Here, I give you this ladder."

"Just listen to us. I mean, how silly can you get. Here I'm sitting in a chair . . ."

"Please, try and stay by the wall. It is not a silly wall but a serious wall. It is serious enough to make you angry for keeping you from the other side. Go back to the wall."

"I got no ladder."

"Do you want the ladder I give you?"

"Alright. But don't watch while I drag-ass up there now."

"I won't . . . Where are you now? . . . Are you doing something?"

"Yes, I'm halfway up the wall, standing here, just standing, and I'm so damn shaky now I don't want to go any higher. I don't want to look over."

"If you don't want to look then come down. Maybe you won't be afraid the next time you go up."

In this instance, the patient's fear to go on with his exploration was a palpable fact. Therefore the therapist gave his support by suggesting a rest. The patient reacted with relief, as if glad to rest after tremendous effort, but then he was also quite excited about the novel exploration of a wall whose existence had not occurred to him until just a short while ago.

He had stayed with the experience of a resistance. He had learned of its guarding quality and he had learned that it was possible to scale this guarding wall, if he wanted to try it again. He was, coincidentally, consumed with a growing curiosity about the sight on the other side of the wall, an excitement and a wish to look further which he had not known before, just as he had not known that he was also afraid to go near his resistance.

Any psychotherapeutic technique can deal with resistances. What distinguishes this one is the degree of the patient's active participation, and therefore the considerable efficiency with which the armor-plating of the neurosis comes under attack.

But our patient has not overcome his wall yet. He said that he was afraid to look. What he has done is to leave the matter lie very much as it has ever since its inception. Existentially speaking, he maintains, with the aid of the resistance, a condition of unfinished business. Historically, he has carried a past event into the present. To finish that business amounts to a destruction of an attachment to the past.

While other aspects of the patient's personality might have kept apace in growth, this attachment—buttressed and guarded—remains a hang-up, a fixation, a thing unaltered by changes in circumstance. We find it altogether helpful to regard resistances as energy in the service of maintaining attachments and fixations, because the focus on our sole therapeutic purpose is in this way kept clear: to liberate the patient.

We are attached to those things that we hold important.

We say that there is no attachment to something which is not important to us. To this extent there is no difference between an attachment to the personal Ferrari and an attachment to the personal wife. The quantitative investment of energy, the concentration on an object, the demand for making the thing one's own, can be equivalent. We point out that this sort of attachment, this possession-minded attachment to an object that attracts, will make objects out of anything desired, be it an inanimate thing or a human being. The man who treats his wife like his car is a possessive fool. The man who treats his car as if it were his wife finds it obviously easier to relate to a machine than to a human being. In that sense, any attachment tends to treat any object solely as more or less of a possession. The wanted car becomes animate, the wanted woman becomes dehumanized.

Both these phenomena of attachment could gain by the Zen doctrine of no-mind—which we might call nonattachment. If the state of no-mind is achieved through the experience of enlightenment called *satori* (mentioned earlier), then the practitioner transcends attachments and becomes free to contact the great oneness which is All.

The process is difficult in our society, and for that matter, we may not even care for that kind of oneness with that kind of All. However, our attachments can be a heavy burden. They can be a crippling drain on our capacity to live here and now. With an attachment to money, a financial setback can destroy a man's reason for being. With an attachment to personal objects, their loss can result in eternal, obsessive ruminations about their replacement. The loss of a person can make suicide plausible. The meaningfulness of life for such a man is as tenuous as his possession of things. But for each attachment which is removed, with each loosening of the hanging-on grip, there is an increment of liberation gained for that person, and a gain in the capacity to relate to another human being which no longer needs to be dehumanized as a possession.

With each resistance dissolved there is a gain in freedom to make or unmake relations by choice. This choice capacity is a goal of therapy.

THE FOCUS TECHNIQUES: THE WORK WITH RESISTANCES

It would seem from much that we have said that techniques are not the sort of thing we care to develop. But we have techniques. We would rather be sensitive enough and spontaneous enough—and both at a high rate of endurance—to make technique redundant. It turns out, in actual practice, that disregard for a modicum of technique, is to insist on failure where failure can be avoided. The point is that techniques are useful sometimes. They can help make contact with a closed patient. They can be useful in helping the patient move ahead. But techniques are only at their best when they are chosen in a relationship of impersonal empathy, when they are the tools which we use while at center. A technique is chosen with timeliness when the therapist is attuned to the patient's condition. The best method flops if used at the wrong time.

We know that the use of a technique is well timed when it works. This is a neat thing to say but it is fairly useless for predictions. We have no predictive rule for the choice of technique in our approach, but we do know when we have chosen best in the past. That was when we were in tune with the patient, when we were not confused by his contradictions or by our own distant drift far from the center. When we have been at out best with inner calm and with outreaching sensitivity then the patient comes across clearly and we see the signs of his readiness: he shows expectation of change. He has the aura of anticipation instead of close guardedness, and there is altogether a sense about him that he looks for something to happen though he has no idea what it is going to be.

This sensing of readiness by the therapist takes practice and exposure. Sometimes we are wrong. The single most telling sign of wrong timing is an increase in resistance. In contrast, the most telling signs of the right timing are these: When the patient asks authentically for help, it is a sign that with assistance he is ready to try what he has not dared to do before. And the time for a technique is always indicated when the patient, as in the earlier example, runs consciously into a block.

These have been general words about techniques and their use. Now here are six specific ways of helping the patient work on his resistances. Please note as we go along that in each instance the technique is primarily something the patient does with himself. It is not so much that the therapist is using a technique as that the patient is learning one.

The Withdrawal Technique

In this technique the patient learns to withdraw *to* himself. This withdrawal is a state of concentration on something he does or feels.

During the session, let us say, the therapist notices that the patient seems to breathe in without breathing out. At any rate, inhalation is noticeable, perhaps because of exaggeration, while the exhale phase is all but unnoticeable. It is possible that the patient communicates that he is attempting to fill up an emptiness in himself. Or the blowing up of the chest is a he-man emphasis, because the patient feels inadequate. There are other possible meanings of the body act. The therapist, at this point, only knows his own impression. He does *not* make an interpretation for the patient. Instead he offers withdrawal technique which calls the patient's own exploration into play. The technique taps the patient's implicit knowledge.

"Please sit back now," says the therapist. "Close your eyes. And now pay attention to your breathing. Feel it. Feel what you do. Is there a difference between breathing in and breathing out?"

Though there is a gradual increase in focus with each concentration aid which the therapist offers, attention is only directed to phenomenological events. Now the therapist falls silent. Any meanings, any projections about the asymmetric breathing rhythm are awaited to come from the patient. *His* meanings are the ones that matter. The revelation of a purpose, if any, in the striking body act of his breathing must come from him.

Hopefully, the patient will make contact with his breathing. Simple promptings can then help him to stay with the breathing awareness. He is urged to look at it, "feel" it, alter it, note how it feels when the habitual way is being nudged into a different rhythm. "How does it feel?" and "What is it doing?" are the sort of direct remarks that characterize the phenomenological level on which the technique operates. Ideations, fantasies, and projections may develop from this soil of experience (we will speak of them later) but these are not an actual part of an exercise designed to regain bodily, sensory awareness.

The withdrawal technique was here used in order to focus on a recognizable, arrhythmic body operation. We have found the same effort productive when applied to a much more amorphous situation, such as the therapeutic impasse.

Both patient and therapist feel that nothing is happening. Everything has been said, nothing new seems to beckon anywhere. Both participants feel a dullness and some boredom.

The mood picture describes a session with a young woman who entered therapy with the presenting complaint of an inability to obtain an orgasm. There was a certain amount of work done which dealt with historical antecedents of her present complaint. Throughout and with increasing facility the patient was able to talk about her lack of sexual feeling. There was no feeling at the labia, at the clitoris, or inside the vagina. The anatomical ranging about and the discussing of feelings or no feelings well-nigh exhausted the repertoire of the human sensorium. It got to be pretty dull and there was nothing to talk about.

"You've talked about what you don't feel," said the therapist. "This time, let's not talk. And this time, just sit with your body and let it talk to you."

"What part?"

"Don't ask. Just listen."

She sat in silence for a while and then reported that she heard humming and strumming going on inside her ears.

"What's it feel like?"

"You said I should listen," was the answer.

"On the other hand," said the therapist, sorry to have been taken so literally about the suggestion of listening, "on the other hand, I did not say you should not sense anything else about your body."

"It is rather difficult to concentrate on the sounds at the moment."

"What interferes?"

"The dominant feeling is in the belly. But that's not anything to listen to."

"Can you stay with the belly?"

In this case there were just a few more assists to help the patient stay with her abdomen for the rest of the session. Her own implicit interest kept her concentration ranging about belly, waist, internal motions, pressures, sensations of heat, and then a sense of constriction. The eventual fantasy which so to speak snapped into place after some free ranging about with sensations was the image of a belt. It cinched her waist. It prevented pelvic motion. It became a rigid band that compressed her belly.

"Describe the belt."

She described physical details of the belt with growing concentration and then, "A chastity belt!" she said.

Three more sessions were spent with the belt in the manner of the withdrawal technique. It was like play, it always became concernful, and then the patient decided to try taking off the belt. She succeeded in "taking it off" at the end of the third session. The immediate sensation was "I feel relaxed and sort of nicely weary. Like after straining and working hard."

The sensation is fairly common after completing withdrawal work. But more significantly, the patient reported during the next session that in the interim she had experienced her first orgasm in years.

The chastity belt, we must add, went back on, and the therapeutic work concerned with the nature of its function and the reasons for its presence continued. But the example of the withdrawal work is given here because it shows how therapeutic work could leave the level of ideations with this technique and could now become a felt experience of just precisely what the patient was doing to herself. Therapy from this point on took the form of learning how to take off the belt, what positive function it served when the patient put it on, and what price she paid for its safety. The patient did her problem solving on an experimental level. She participated in her cure on the sensory plane where, so to speak, the action was.

In our experience the withdrawal technique is a relatively simple task for neurotics who have retained a fair measure of integration in their personality. The same is not true in the case of borderline psychotics and particularly in work with schizophrenic patients. In such cases withdrawal as a technique is quite difficult and, in the patient's experience, often frightening. But in the case of patients who have retained some measure of good contact with themselves the withdrawal technique, though simple, can do an otherwise complex job of promoting insight with remarkable dispatch. This includes such despairing prospects as the woman who had been in continuous psychotherapy with a variety of therapists for over nine years.

She had a good "intellectual" understanding of her problems and she understood their meaning according to several theories. The patient's nine-year education had promoted a succinct, verbal skill, and she was so wise in the ways of techniques that she wondered if there could ever be anything else that was new under the sun. Not surprisingly at all, the patient had about as much bodily awareness as a block of wood. We are describing this additional instance of withdrawal work because it illustrates more dramatically than the first how the technique will tap ever new sources of experience in the patient.

We asked the patient to withdraw, as described above. Though this was her first attempt to range with awareness over her body, she complied with trained alacrity and with the full knowledge that none of this would of course lead any place where she had not been before.

The patient very quickly found herself where she wanted to be the least. Her intellectual presence became tenuous, cloudy, and shot through with confusion. She was asked to stay with the confusion. She then bore the extreme discomfort of the state with the help of the therapist's presence. The therapist told the patient to give herself comfort in any way she saw fit, but to stay with the confusion instead of shutting it out. The patient did a number of spontaneous things, such as altering her breathing, placing her palms protectively over the skull, rocking back and forth on occasion—in any event, the confusion subsided after a while. She was now told to stay with that changing sensation too. The change was from splintered focus (confusion) toward a gathering focus (concentration on a newly emerging view.)

She became aware of a sensation in her abdomen. She had not experienced it before, she reported. "Let it come to you," said the therapist "Don't mess with it at all. Just feel it out."

She paid attention to her abdominal sensation for a good time, aware now of the fact that the sensation waxed, waned, moved, and resettled it-self. She was encouraged to attend to the sensation without any attempt to understand it or to explain it. In this way she then came to describe the sensation of a wound made by a knife.

"Stay with it." The knife was still in her abdomen. Then came more detail. The blade had a triangular shape.

We point out that here was the moment for a telling interpretation: The symbolism of the triangle, the triangular relationship which in fact existed between this patient and her mother and father in a classic oedipal sense, but this therapist (not the writer, in this case) did not want to stimu-late the young woman's proclivity for intellectual sport with dynamics. No interpretation was offered.

To repeat, the patient's experiencing is needed, not the explaining.

The knife and the wound exist for this patient. They are as real for her at this moment as the chair she sits in. The knife is not a metaphor until it is used as a metaphor. The experience is not a symbol until it is used as such. The imagery of the knife, as it occurs, as it is maintained, is the ex-perience as such. This experience is the phenomenon we want to work with at this point.

Please note that we are not saying that there is no symbolism involved in the case of the triangular knife. We think there is. Our point is that we are taking the long way around if we work through the interpretation of the symbolism in this case.

As might be expected, our young woman was highly astonished to find that she "had been carrying this experience around" all this time. Also, to no one's surprise, our wised-up patient instantly started to move away from the experience in her abdomen by intoning a veritable symphony of interpretations of knife-type characteristics.

The therapist ignored the young woman's interpretations. When she had run down somewhat he asked her to describe the experience of the knife itself but in detail.

She reentered the phenomenological world of her body experience and in the course of resulting fantasy discovered that she could not remove the knife, and that this was true because she did not want to touch the gore on the hilt of the knife. She was incapable of action because of an over-whelming disgust.

Therapeutic work now stayed with the experience of disgust. A vital factor in this patient's neurotic structure had been discovered for the first time. If became the subject of work. The phase of this case mentioned here is meant to demonstrate how the withdrawal technique became like the tapping of a long-forgotten fount of unused knowledge.

We go to the sine qua non source of resistance experience, the sen-sations. This is the body language. We follow the patient's work, as sen-sations are then used in the making of fantasies. We note how the fantasies, used existentially and without interpretation, are the patient's delivery of how he attempts to get done with his unfinished business. This work is diagnostic as it shows *how* the patient does *what*. The work is therapeutic because the patient reengages in new solutions.

It is a shame that such a fine, simple method has drawbacks, but it does. These drawbacks are the shortcomings of the therapist.

The withdrawal technique, as well as all the other focus techniques which we will describe, does not work if the therapist has not learned how to observe sensitively when a situation is in change for the patient. There is no such thing as hauling the method out and putting it into the session with a hearty, "Now let's use this one." If the patient is on an extrovert kick of ebullience or sheer theatrics, and if all that overt demonstrating has the vital purpose of dissipating a surcharge of tension, then there is no productive point to the suggestion that the patient quietly turn inward and contemplate the touch of some shy nerve-flutterings somewhere within. The example is exaggerated and would require no sensitive tuning in. But the exaggeration points up the need to gauge the demands of the technique against the current state of the patient.

Once the right moment for the onset of the technique has been found, then the chief source of its possible misuse is impatience on the part of the therapist.

The patient must be allowed to work the method without any push from the therapist for more speed. There are typical signs in the therapist who is getting ready to spoil the technique. He starts feeling that he now must do something. He is suddenly possessed with the knowledge that he himself has right now an experience which the patient should be having. Those are the signs of taking over. But the withdrawal work of the patient cannot be taken over.

The method does not work when an experience is suggested to the patient. He must find one, any one, himself. The patient can be introduced to the withdrawal technique, but if the content of its use is also given, the purpose of the technique has been missed.

The patient may withdraw to his body and find nothing but a rapidly beating heart. Notwithstanding the therapist's knowledge that there is a shoulder cramp which must eventually be considered, the patient is now looking at the heart. Stay with it. What is it doing? What does it want to do? Does it make a sound, does the sound say anything to you? Again, these are samples of the kind of phenomenological focus that goes to the somatic locus of sensations and allows the basic body language finally to say something over the chronic din of conceptualizing.

Typically in the early stages of therapy the patient reports that he feels nothing while using the technique. The next step is in line with everything we have said on the subject: Stay with "nothingness."

It may turn out to be the nothingness of his unawareness which may go with a healthy body, or it may turn out to be the desensitization of his resistance itself. Nobody knows ahead of time. But to stay with the focus that comes up will check out the eventual meaning of the awareness question.

Many people in our culture are estranged from their own bodies and from an identification with their own body experience. They view their body as a thing. The withdrawal technique will again let them experience the body as "This is I, "instead of some sort of "it" over there.

No part of this technique and its use is meant as a paean for constant surveillance and inspection of all the nuances of the self. Please do not forget that we are describing an action in the context of very special conditions: Something has gone wrong. The harmony of the person is tilted by malfunctions.

I do not pay any special attention to my hand while it is working well. I am not even aware of its presence. But when it is cut, when it bleeds, when it hurts to do what I want to do. . . .

One general reminder that applies to all the focus techniques: Once the patient knows them, he can use them alone. Remember the homework suggestion we have made. Any and all the techniques in this section lend themselves well to the work of therapy, a task that is best not confined to the speciality place of a session.

The Image Technique

This method is identical to the withdrawal technique, except that the focus of attention does not range over body sensations but falls on imagery. (The previous examples of withdrawal work have shown how one technique inevitably flows into the other.)

Before giving descriptions and examples of image work we must make a working distinction between projections and fantasies.

The production of fantasy and of projection may look the same at first blush. Both are visual constructions, both have shapes, colors, forms in truly infinite variety. But we must draw the distinction between them because the image technique works with fantasy only.

We will deal with projections later. They are the red meat in the teeth of therapeutic work, marked by an unmalleable, fixed quality which is no longer under volitional control. Projections are phenomenological realities that are instrumental parts of a person's world. They are maintained as realities, regardless of their conflict with events that occur outside of the person. Projections are a severely serious business because their possible death would seem tantamount to the destruction of the individual.

None of this describes a fantasy. In contrast to projections, a fantasy is almost a playful thing. It is under the image maker's control to a very large extent, and its very volatility is evidence of the much lighter affective investment. While a projection stands for nothing but itself, a fantasy can assume substitute functions. It can stand for something else, as in the case of a symbol, or it can make up for a lack, as is the case in the daydream. The fantasy is responsive to mood, and intent, and is the very stuff of which imaginative problem solving is made. Predictably, the image technique has here a versatile human capacity at its disposal.

As in the work with the withdrawal technique, we would ask the patient to make himself comfortable. Then we ask him to close his eyes, an instruction that is not as important in the previous technique but is very instrumental with visual imagery. Then the direction is to pay attention to any visual images which might arise: Watch what you see, look around there, range about, and allow forms to come clear.

In contrast to the work with body sensations, there is considerably more variety in visual constructions. For that reason there is no way of predicting at all what will come up with the use of the image technique.

Frequently the kind of thing that is visually produced reflects rather clearly the patient's immediate sense of lack in himself. This is particularly true when the method is used to break an impasse. A compulsive patient, for example, reported a persistent image of an unopened rose.

"Stay with it. How would you describe it to me?"

"It's closed. It's a bud, actually. Tightly closed. You know. Not ready to open."

"Fine. Just keep watching it for a while."

This was the wrong thing to say, as it turned out. This compulsive just kept watching the tightly closed rose and introduced no movement whatsoever into the imagery. In a while, careful not to suggest what ought to be seen, the therapist took a more active role.

"What can we do together with that rose?"

"Uh, well looking at it won't do it."

"Do something else."

This took some work, but the rose, by and by, was made to open. (This patient's choice was to ask the therapist for the use of a watering can.)

The point in this sample of the image technique is to show how the rose, as a particular illustration of one of the patient's particular qualities, became a tool for work on the patient's tightness. This fifteen-minute instance of opening up a rose did not remove the patient's quality of closedness toward his life experience. However, he now confronted the task and he now knew it to be a task. He applied himself to a purpose and he discovered his wish to be open. He returned to the image technique for several sessions and allowed himself to become quite enchanted with the image of the flower and with his own contemplations on the beauty of openness. The image technique reintroduced him to the wish for openness, a realm of life which had almost atrophied for him.

The imagery developed under this technique may be simple, such as seeing no more than a chair, or it may be complex, involving action of people and fantasies about their various moods. The manner of working with the technique is the same in simple as well as in complex imagery.

We ask for images. We allow them to be unfolded and we encourage descriptions of detail which go beyond the mere statement of the initial view.

We have found that the heightened involvement entailed by full-detail descriptions makes the patient that much more accessible to the work with the fantasies that must follow their production. One final note. The technique, as in the case with withdrawal, is negated when the therapist participates in the production of fantasy. Therefore the therapist does not join in the work on the material until the patient is done describing his images in detail.

The Technique of the Double Bind

We introduce this technique with a warning. Its curative strength can hurt more than the disorder which it is meant to correct. The double bind can do damage.

This powerful technique is not recommended for the inexperienced therapist, nor is it for those days of work when the therapist does not feel kindly.

The double bind is the Hobson's choice of psychotherapy. A situation is posed in which no choice is right.

In effect, two results are demanded of one act, and one result denies the other. The dilemma is common enough. A wife makes the plaint. "Why don't you make more money so that we can spend more time together?" She has now set the husband up to be a loser. If he tries to make more money it will mean he must spend less time with her. If he spends more time with her, then he will make less money.

In the psychopathology of everyday life there are more stringent examples. A clinging mother turns ill at the prospect of her daughter's marriage. "Go, dear. I want your happiness. And don't worry. I'll try and manage by myself somehow."

If the daughter leaves, she is the loser through guilt. If she stays, she is the loser through resentment.

While the frustrations of the double bind are frequent enough in common encounters, they are most definitely built into the psychotherapeutic situation. We make the point to reemphasize that the intentional use of the double bind (we will come to its use in a moment) requires not just a cautious but an experienced hand.

As for the built-in double bind of the therapeutic situation: On one hand the therapist tells the patient that he accepts him as he is; on the other, he wants him to change. But it gets worse. The therapist performs his work through genuine sharing and with human compassion. But while he establishes a relationship that contains all the qualities of friendship and affection, he is as likely as not to see the patient only in the office. On top of that, he asks to be paid for all this, and what's worse, he establishes this relationship with anyone who has the money.

Whether viewed wisely or not, the physical facts of the therapeutic situation lend themselves to doubts by the patient. Add to that the punishing qualities of the double bind which is intentionally poised at the patient's innards, and the use of the technique must remain a restricted thing.

The essential quality which is introduced by the technique is confusion. The double bind clubs the patient brutally into a corner from which every exit is failure.

Then why use it?

Because there is a type of patient whose inexorable character rigidity will not break, except under the blow of the double bind. The compulsive patient is just one example, but there are many patients whose steel-frame character yoke will not give under any other technique.

The one adequate response to the double bind is to refuse it.

"Have you stopped beating your wife?" The question deserves no answer. It requires merely a comment.

"I won't answer because you have asked a pseudoquestion. You have in fact made an assertion which is only dressed up as a question." And so the double bind has been adroitly beaten.

But this sort of agility of using an objective response to a loaded question is not easy for the rigid patient. The person whose life mode has become an arsenal of ever-ready, ever-available means of defense *is* the one who takes any attack seriously and literally. When faced with a double bind he will apply himself with utter solemnity to each one of the contradictory propositions. This means, of course, that he is already caught. For this reason the patient with the most ironclad character structure is precisely the one who will get most deeply involved in the dilemma of the double bind. He is the patient to whom we restrict the use of this trap. No one who accepts the double bind wins, but the rigid and rule-ridden character is its most obliging victim. Since not much else will penetrate his structure, we reserve cautious use of the technique to him.

The chronic double bind is a pathogen of schizophrenia. The therapeutic double bind, in contrast, is applied only in short instances, so that there is relief. Both the therapeutic and the pathogenic variety are contained in the following summary of a number of sessions:

A middle-age couple had a schizophrenic son in the state hospital. The couple came jointly into therapy because they had been advised by their son's psychiatrist that they too could use help.

The session started significantly enough. The father said something innocuous when the mother, like a shot, made a querulous accusation.

"I just want you to know that he never says what he really means."

Now the father assumed his customary role, ostensibly in an effort to mollify.

"Well," he said to the therapist. "She and I sometimes don't get along.

"You see?" There he did it again, not telling the whole of it!" supplied the distaff player.

The father supplied his required contribution to the making of the double bind. He started to yell.

"If you really want the truth, woman, I'll just plain say it: You just plain make me sick!"

Now the mother had him in the customary corner. As becomes a victor, her delivery was calm and dignified.

"You can see," she said to the therapist, "why our son is sick. My husband always talks like that."

Next, the father changes tactics. He is not going to be trapped that way again. Instead of shouting and saying things, he becomes increasingly silent and morose during the session. Naturally, his wife is quite up to that simple maneuver.

"And that's another thing," she explains to the therapist. "If he'd take a more active part in things, we'd have a better relationship." and ad nauseam. . . .

As a point in fact, the mother had subjected her son to the unrelieved double binding which she demonstrated in the sessions. As part of the same constellation, the father would work his tortured anger out on the son. As a result, the boy could never get close to the father and was constrained to go for everything to the mother. What the mother gave him with her formula for preordained failure was then the ultimate bludgeoning that drove the son to the asylum.

Neither parent was particularly compulsive, but the rigidity of their views and the immutability of their habitual reactions made them precisely the types for the therapeutic use of the double bind. The technique simply amounted to turning the tables on them.

The therapist said to the father: "Come to think of it, it's a healthy thing to swear at your wife now and then. Matter of fact, do it more often."

The effect on the father was that he ceased being the loser. Now when he swore at his wife, he had the therapist's approval. Simultaneously, the therapist put the double bind on the wife.

She had to approve of her husband's swearing, but her husband's swearing in turn was the thing that promoted the sickness of the son!

In the context of the sessions, this became precisely the dilemma she had to grapple with. Her new position upset her tremendously. None of the formulas worked anymore. The character fissured. There was genuine anxiety. Only now, after the double-bind bludgeoning, could therapeutic work toward growth take place.

But we opened with a warning and we will close with it: The double bind is such a big stick that its use requires a great deal of compassion. As for use in homework, those who can use it on themselves are either too nice for it, or quite healthy.

The Shuttle Technique

The shuttle technique is a role-playing fantasy in which the patient dramatizes both sides of a conflict. We like the technique because it impinges directly upon one of the main, structural characteristics of the neurosis, the personality split. The shuttle technique produces a dialogue between the split parts of the personality.

The split describes the condition in which part of the person is the acknowledged self and the other part is the unwanted aspect, which is walled off from awareness by the desensitization of our resistances. Every split, in that sense, represents unfinished business and its maintainence in the psychological make-up demands that we make do with some fragmentary state of integration. In this state the unacknowledged aspect of the self is dragged along like dead weight. That dead weight, when it rises into some sort of awareness, is the enemy. The shuttle technique helps us meet our unwanted self.

A young married man of twenty-six, in therapy because of some marital difficulties, is a case in point. He has grown to manhood with a hang-up of unfinished business in regard to his mother. The mother's personal, active influence has largely ceased, but the patient's reaction to the mother remains as an active, self-generated charge of resentment in him. He never has and he does not now express his anger toward her. Typically enough, he has no notion of the son-anger, the grown-up resentment, and its active direction, namely our patient's private mother image. Symptomatically, he reads "mother" into any hapless victim with the slightest resemblance to the mother qualities which upset him. The repository for his projections about mother, the patient's young wife in this case, need say no more than, "Don't forget your umbrella," and the mother mirage then gets a surcharge of dislike for all the sins which mother mirages are heir to. As for the therapeutic situation, this unfinished business of resentment is activated any time the patient finds that the therapist is "mothering" him.

A psychoanalytic orientation may well favor the relevant interpretation at this point. "You are not angry with me, actually. You are angry with your mother."

From our point of view this is not an efficient way of handling the patient's misplaced attentions. The interpretation promotes the patient's intellectual insight into a situation which is badly lacking in experiential referents. The patient has neither experienced his anger nor its direction. Therefore we now use the shuttle technique.

"You find that I'm mothering you. Alright. I'm now mothering you and you give your answer."

"You're not my mother. She's quite something else again, let me tell you. She's—anyway. Quite different."

"You know what she's like."

"Of course."

"Then let's have her in that chair there. Imagine she's sitting there. Look at her. You see her?"

In a while, with a nudge to describe the mother—a controlled image technique, so to speak—the patient projects the mother into the chair and sees her. This young man made that quite clear with the glowering expression on his face.

"Tell her what you think of her mothering you. Go ahead."

"Uh—look, mother. I know all about umbrellas, you know. So there's no need to tell me about it. Uh, over and over."

"What does she say?"

"Huh?"

"Look at her. What does she say."

"Nothing. No need to say anything with *that* expression on her face. That's the expression which says with one sad, suffering look, how I'm forgetting that all this is for my own mother—for my own good."

"What do you think of that?"

"I'll tell you what I think of that. She . . . "

"Don't tell me. Tell her."

"Alright!"

And in this manner the patient is helped to confront his projection of "mother," to engage in dialogue, to enter the experience of one of those unfinished encounters he has never allowed to come to a head. In the shuttle technique he is not in the customary situation in which he dribbles off his resentment toward substitute objects. He now confronts his projection directly.

In a surprisingly quick and thorough manner the technique leads the patient into a number of experiences. He learns to know the projection he is carrying about with himself. He gets acquainted with an aspect of his being whose existence he has largely ignored and denied. He engages in his own argument of rationalizations, reasons, and logical tricks, a demonstration that can go a long way toward knowing the sound of one's real emotions. The dialogue in the shuttle technique makes known the layers of self-deceptions and excuses that guard the blunt simplicity of a hidden wish. The technique reopens the matter of unfinished business and, in its pursuit, finishes it. The split can heal. The person becomes whole again.

The manifest split which the patient maintains may not take the shape and form of a projected person. A 19-year old male patient with vague complaints of anxiety, estrangement, *Weltschmerz*, and a feeling of drabness about everything, brought with him an unacknowledged split that was no more than a sound in the head. The discovery of the split began by paying attention to the patient's phenomenological manner of being in therapy. A tape of part of the instrumental session shows how the shuttle technique was introduced.

"You don't look like you're listening to me," said the therapist.

"Sorry. I can hear you."

"What did you hear?"

"—What? About the session. The one I missed."

The therapist waited. Then the patient finished.

"Well, I frankly just didn't care. I didn't care coming here." And when the young man had said that his face went blank and he seemed to be less in the room than before.

"Where are you?" said the therapist.

"Silly question."

"And what are you doing?"

There came a shrug. Its quality was more of distraction than of dismissal.

"I'm listening," said the patient.

"Yes. What do you hear is what I'm asking you."

The patient had gone dead and distant at points of anxiety before. This moment's blankness of expression was a case in point. Now the therapist wished to stay with that moment.

"Tell me what you are listening to now."

And then the patient described the sound in his head. He had it often and it became loud and insistent at moments of stress, like this one.

"Can you let me hear it?" asked the therapist, and with this invitation to speak or to sound like the split-off part of himself the patient was introduced to the dialogue of the shuttle technique. In a moment he agreed to express the sound in his head, explaining that he could do it best on his flute.

He brought his flute to the next session. He listened to the sounds in his head and then, for most of the hour, he played—he expressed what he heard on his flute. When he put the instrument down his mien and his carriage conveyed his sense of presence.

"I played it," he said, and then. "I played *my* sound!"

The split had been joined. There was no longer *it* buzzing at him but *he* had acknowledged the sound as his own.

The symptom never recurred, and only after its dissipation was the patient able to hear the therapist. The duration of work, in this instance, extended over no more than a dozen sessions. It was rather happy work.

The dialogue between split parts of oneself can be explicitly in the first person. "A part of me wants to die. I want to kill myself. And a part of me wants to live."

We put this patient in the two chairs in the office. He demonstrated his current perference by making himself the one who wished to live and put his projection of himself, the one who wanted to be dead, in the other chair. These two were now encouraged to talk to each other.

But the dialogue of "I want to live and "I want to die" came across with all the fervor of an accountant reading a client's profit-and-loss sheet. In this case, there was no inspired trick to turn the dull tide, there was no sudden decision on the part of the patient to say something heartfelt to his alter ego. We mentioned this case because sometimes the shuttle technique simply takes dogged time. The therapist's job in the shuttle technique is to stage-set as best he can and then, like Stanislavski, turn his man loose as soon as the patient has become that part which he is enacting. The contradictory feelings of this patient remained on the level of verbal platitudes for a number of sessions but then, perhaps out of no more than bored exasperation, the patient commenced to be each part, to experience each of him with emotion. When the splits made contact in his operation of becoming both again, the healing began with that contact.

We have distinguished earlier between fantasies and projections, and then pointed out that the image technique utilizes largely fantasies. In contrast, the shuttle technique lends itself best to work with projections, those fixed images of ourselves which are the cast-out fragments that plague us because we will not acknowledge them. The shuttle technique helps contact those rejects of ourselves, and helps us acknowledge them. This is mentioned only in passing; we will speak of projections again.

To return to homework once more: The shuttle technique, in contrast to the double-bind catastrophe, is a good exercise to practice and use when alone.

The Mourning Technique

This is a special case of the shuttle technique. Again, the patient is asked to concentrate on a well-formed projection and to relate its description to the therapist. But in this instance the purpose of the method is specifically directed. The earlier examples of the shuttle technique showed the versatile use of the dialogue with projections. In the special case of the mourning technique the patient is asked to raise his ghosts in order to exorcise and to destroy them.

Only the occasional person has not had a death in the family. Almost everyone has had to give up a relationship at one time or another without being ready for the separation. Some cultures appreciate the strains of personal loss and provide rituals that promote the mourning experience; this event of living through the sense of loss puts an end to the attachment to an object now dead and gone. There is the ritual use of professional mourners in Mediterranian cultures. They howl their grief for all to share. The New Orleans tradition of the funeral dirge played by the musicians who follow the coffin is another example. The completion of mourning, the cutting of the bond, is then dramatically expressed when the same musicians return from the graveyard, playing their happy and capricious jazz improvisations. The German *Leichenschmaus*, the gluttonous eating feast after burying the dead, is another avowal that the separation between life and death truly exists. The Seminoles leave a personal gift with their dead, which in their case is a real act of giving something up. In contrast, our own sentimental cults that promote a fake permanence of the loved one, that paint the cadever of our loss into some parody of eternal life, actually inhibit the true sensations of loss—grief and mourning.

The psychic strain of perpetuating an attachment to what is now an illusion can drain the living in order to keep the dead alive. We either mourn and bury our dead, or live haunted by ghosts.

Ghosts exist. We know nothing about disembodied wraiths, but we do know the ghosts that the patient harbors. We know these illusions of permanence that he maintains for some measure of static comfort, for whose life he pays by living a little bit less.

There is no significant difference between the mourning technique and the shuttle method, except for the specificity of the aim. We chiefly made mourning a separate section because we think it worthwhile that the therapist look for the ghost in his patient's life.

We saw a minister for a series of sessions who worked very successfully in many ways. He engaged with his multileveled ambivalence problems in regard to his father, his mother, and a number of other people. He worked through many resistances, revitalized dead spots, and redintegrated in a wonderful way. Nevertheless he maintained a lingering sense that all was not well. The state was incomprehensible until we found his ghost.

We sat with him and his vague sense of incompletion for several sessions without gaining an inch. The patient could not focus on anything clearly, he could not specify just what it was that he felt. Part of the recording of the patient's engagement with his ghost runs like this.

"Alright," said the therapist. "Whatever it is, let's try this. Put it in the other room."

"What room?"

"Put it behind the wall there and let it be there in the room behind the wall."

"Oh. Very good. I'll try that. I'll have to close my eyes and— yes, I'll try that."

There was some postural shifting, quietness, some purposeful breathing.

"Can you tell me what goes on?" asked the therapist in a while.

"It's in the other room. I'm sitting here sensing about, feeling around and so forth trying to learn what it is there, in that room."

In a while, "Let it tell you, instead."

"Alright. I'm just sitting here listening for it, letting—Yes!"

As it turned out, something took shape now for the patient, an event which showed so far only in his intentness and excitement. Then:

"It's there, in the room, but what?"

"Let me help you. Is it a person?"

"Yes."

"Tell me how you know the person is there."

"I can hear it now! I hear the voice—talking, talking to me. I can't tell what he says, but he's talking to me."

"Who?"

"The voice—it's my father!"

The events, though specific, show the progressive focusing on a projection which is rather usual with the technique. Also fairly common is the fact that the identification of the projection in and of itself did not produce any relief in the patient. Wonderment, yes, but, so far no relief. However, now there was an object for confrontation.

The patient's real father was dead and the subsequent work of dialogue with the projection became a dramatic enactment of the various attitudinal things that the patient did to keep his father alive. He learned that he did not want his father to be dead.

Subsequent therapy was designed to help the patient say good-bye. In the case of this minister the most natural thing was to have him perform the burial rites. When he had done this, he had laid his ghost to rest.

The Exaggeration Technique

Of all the focus techniques which we have described, this is the only one which does not work explicitly with the patient's fantasies or with his projections. Instead, the exaggeration technique works with the patient's actual behavior.

Essentially, we see what the patient does and then we help him experience his *modus operandi* by asking him to exaggerate it. The exaggeration can range in its form from a parody of the behavior itself to an enactment of its precise opposite. Sometimes the patient can be put on the receiving end of his behavior and the therapist will mimic what the patient is doing.

In any event, it is the purpose of the technique to make the experience of a habitual behavior device unavoidable. Once the recognition of the behavior blind spot has been achieved, and not before, can the work on its meaning and purpose commence.

The technique applies to automatic behaviors. The integrated person has habits that save time and effort, but their use remains flexible and appropriate to the unique demands of a new situation. In contrast, the neurotic tends to use his habits because he has got them, and not because they fit changing demands. He will respond with his neurosis regardless of circumstances. Diagnostically, the neurotic is predictable. This includes what he will do, plus the fact that it will be inappropriate a good deal of the time.

The passive-dependent personality is an example. (We would not be able to type him if he were not consistent.) He makes each session very quickly into a tableau of the supplicant at the knee of the oracle. The habit is fixed and there is no use talking about it. But perhaps it can be shown. The following paraphrased tape recording is a demonstration of that.

"I'm going to the football game this week-end, " opens the patient.

"Ah."

" 'Ah' nothing. I wish it were that simple."

Methinks: here it comes. I am only going to say "Hm" for a while.

"Hm is right," says the patient with fine show of preoccupied problem solving. The problem, in the meantime, turns out to be how to snag the therapist into solving a problem for him. "My wife doesn't like football, you know."

"She's not going?"

"You don't get it. She'd go and I'd like her to go. I like spending time with her and she wants to spend time with me but she'd rather do it at home, spend time is what I'm talking about, and not on some hard bench grumbling about the weather with some padded gorillas running around in the mud. That's all it means to her. I like her to have fun too. You know that."

"At home."

"But for her to sit home alone and me at the football game? I really want to go to that game. How do you convince a woman, huh? I mean if you were in my place?"

"In your place, I wouldn't know what to do."

"What's that ? I mean, hell man, if you really wanted to go!"

"I wouldn't want my wife to be all alone and no fun at home. You know how it is."

"Yeah."

He does not get a thing out of this exchange. He wants to be told what to do but instead his own decision is fed back to him. There is no help from the oracle, and there is no understanding by the supplicant. But now, while his intent remains infantile, his method begins to show new finesse.

"She knows all about you," and he smiles.

I smile.

"She knows I tell you everything and how you've helped me. She actually thinks a hell of a lot of you."

"What happened to the football game? I'm still thinking about . . ."

"Me too," he says and the way he hitches around in his chair looks either like the cat is getting ready to jump the mouse or he's going to do me a favor now and sell me the Brooklyn Bridge. "You like football, don't you?"

"Yes."

"You want to go to the game this weekend? Look, you know what we could do? You could, I mean, we could go . . ."

"Wait a minute." It was time. He was not usurping the authority of the oracle. He was coercing it. The time had come for some finesse in the other direction. "I really would love to go, but I have to ask my boss."

"Ask your boss? Are you nuts?"

"I got work to get out for the clinic and it's got to be done by the end of the weekend. I don't know what to tell my boss, if I can't deliver because I went to a football game. I mean, you've got experience with this sort of thing. How would you do it?"

"Now let me get this. You mean you're afraid of him?"

"I don't want to disappoint him and I don't want to miss the game. Help me."

"I should help *you*? Man, you're here to help *me*!"

"You won't take over for me?"

"What goes on here, for crying out loud!"

"You just asked me to take over for you. That's what just went on here."

When the shoe was put on the other foot the patient ended up at the receiving end of his own devices. He saw what it was like. He had experienced the manipulation. The technique, which we will call opposite exaggeration, became a first contact with a habit which he had used quite universally and quite unbeknown to himself. His awareness was increased. His first step toward behavior choice had been taken.

The exaggeration technique also lends itself to a recognition or pervasive attitudes which are not as directly manipulatory as in the previous example. Nevertheless, a more covert attitude can also be a habitual manner of treating the world.

He talks and we listen. It may take a few hours but then, for example, the therapist hears the persistent nagging sound in the background.

"I hear you nagging. Do you hear it?"

"Hear what? I know what I was saying but you keep interrupting me. I realize this is kind of complicated and of course I don't know the kind of words you use, but all that means, seems to me, you should be listening and not interrupting with things that have nothing to do with the subject. I don't think you're even paying attention now. Maybe if you sat with your hands away from your face like that. The other day you did the same thing. I even told you then. If you're going to be of any help—Well, what's the use."

"Did you hear your tone of voice?"

"Of course I heard my tone of voice. *I* listen."

"Then do it again for me, please. Same tone of voice."

"I said that I have a problem expressing myself. And I asked how you might help me."

"I didn't hear the same tone of voice. Did you?"

In a moment the patient smiled with a touch of embarrassment and said no, it wasn't quite the same thing.

"If you'd let me try it the way I heard it, do you think you might recognize it?"

The patient, with a touch of good sportsmanship, gave permission. It is important that the patient agrees to the switch in this case, or else he will not really listen. It is doubly important that the therapist forgo this golden chance of making fun of the patient and of paying him back for the hours of unrelieved nagging. We would remind at this point of the attitude which makes for a confrontive, therapeutic encounter: impersonal empathy, which means a regard for the other, uncolored by feelings oriented toward judgments of what is seen, feelings that restrict the view to dimensions of worth, danger, and usefulness. This means that the therapist had better not play this game unless he feels well centered.

But now he feels well put together, he can see the patient who sits and awaits with a touch of partly amused, partly apprehensive curiosity, the same one who can also nag. Which is the aspect that is now going to be fed back to him?

"Well, if you'd be a little more considerate of what I'm going through here you'd try and say things a little more straight, a little less bent like little hooks to get into me, if you know what I mean. And I'm telling you this only because I know you've got the stuff to be straight with me. I don't know why you don't try. I wish you'd really try your best sometime and not leave it all up to me. You'd get what I'm trying to do here. Maybe you're trying not to get it. If you were really the sort of person who'd . . . "

"Enough! I get it!"

It is possible, of course, that the patient gets too much and flees behind a barricade of justifications, complaints, and a renewed drip treatment of one little niggling demand after another. Watch the patient. Never get so carried away with the performance so as to lose touch with the audience. You might to continue to talk to a nagger and end up by looking at a self-righteous maniac.

It is altogether well to remember that no matter in what way the focus techniques are employed, they are all designed for use toward one end: To put the patient in touch with areas in himself whose existence he must learn to know and accept if he wants psychological harmony. We are working to increase the range of his behavioral choice. We are trying to restore his own self-command in place of a malfunction that has started to operate independently.

The patient's hands shake. A fluttery, shaking sensation possesses his innards. It seems to come from nowhere and it is beyond his powers of control. Simply on the basis of experience we recognize the symptom as a somatic expression of an anxiety state. But the patient does not know this. In fact, the very fact that the anxiety spills over into somatic form seems to decrease or entirely obliterate any anxiety feeling as such. The patient is not in touch with his symptom. *It* shakes, and it means nothing to him.

The exaggeration technique can jack up the intensity of the symptom. Then it will talk louder to him.

"I got this shaking. Look at my hands. It doesn't seem to mean anything but here it comes. I just want to ge rid of it, forget it."

"Before you can forget it, you will have to learn what it is you are trying to forget; what you are trying to ignore, as I would put it."

"I can't ignore it."

"I know. So right now let's find out what won't let itself be ignored."

We use the "it" language deliberately. It is the language of the patient's choice for the moment. He understands it in safety.

"Instead of ignoring it, let's now pay attention to it."

"It'll get worse."

"Good. It's the way it will tell you more. Try this. Turn to the trembling—let it get bigger—now exaggerate it—is it growing? Make it grow—or let it do what it wants for the moment—"

The presence of the therapist can be reassuring now. In most cases involving accentuation of anxiety symptoms the patient will bear it better by knowing that the therapist attends him with warmth. When the patient comes to the point where he can allow the trembling to grow very strong, then the shut-off feeling-tone will begin to return. He feels anxiety.

Once the patient is aware of this aimless fright, the therapist must contribute again. The specificity of the physical symptoms lends itself well to the chore of finding a meaning in the nonspecific state of anxiety. While the patient is alive now with aimless push in him we attend him so that he might discover experientially what that truncated expression in his hand might be all about: The hand-trembling becomes a violent gesture of shaking filth off his hand; the tremble was the leftover gesture when he interrupted withdrawing in fright. Whatever it was, now the patient will be able to tell.

When exaggerated behavior is the starting point of inquiry; we have found that an opposite exaggeration can bring the purpose of the behavior into awareness. This form of exaggeration technique is particularly indicated when the one-sidedness of the patient is matched by a marked blindness of the opposite.

Our use of opposites is somewhat similar to Frankl's "paradoxical intention," since in both instances we are dealing with so-called negative practice in which the exaggeration of an error promotes the learning of the correct way. By becoming more fully aware of what you want to avoid (the error) you learn its opposite by sharp contrast. In practice and for our purposes, we will now simply turn the patient upside down.

Here is a man who claims to be totally stumped by his wife's behavior. He cannot understand her. He does not understand women at all, by his own account. He also cued the therapist to his interest by opposite emphasis. The patient placed great stress on being a man, a complete man. He had derogatory things to say about such things as acting sissified, weepy, and weak.

The exaggeration technique concentrated on the opposite of his known identification. As a first step he was asked to imitate his wife's conversation, next her conversational manner, and then her manner of deportment and movement in general. Going at a relatively slow pace, in this instance, the patient was gradually led toward efforts to fantasize himself as a woman, to dress like a woman, to give himself a woman's body. As might be expected at various points in this development the patient experienced considerable anxiety. In each instance we encouraged him to exaggerate it, to allow it to point in its chosen direction. Just as often he brought up strong resistances.

Now that the exaggeration technique has defined the area of lack, we work with the resistance in that area exactly as discussed earlier. We do not go behind it. We stay with the phenomenon which exists for the patient with immediacy.

We had a patient for whom nothing existed with very much immediacy. She was a 26-year-old graduate student in psychology, she knew a great deal, and she could not get involved in any meaningful relationships. That was her complaint. "I try," she said. "I know the necessity for a positive attitudinal set, if there is to be any sense of meaningfulness in the social matrix with which we surround ourselves— however, in spite of all the self-realization techniques available to me at my point of development I simply do not seem to be able to make even the simplest contact without that sense of sham and hollowness about it."

The agility of her vocabulary was in sharp contrast to the small, constrained movements in her hands and arms. We suspected another contrast: possibly the unobtrusive movements of her hands and arms were more meaningful than her demonstrative talk.

We began by diverting her attention from conceptual gymnastics to the inactivity of her limbs. The patient began to pay attention to the constraint in her movements. She paid attention to her arms and felt heaviness. Next came the exaggeration of what she felt in her arms and what she did with her arms. The motion in arms and hands ceased altogether. Her report was this: "They are heavy like stones. They are hard, cold, dead, like stone and just stay that way. I can't use them for anything. And who in hell would want to touch that?"

Her distance from others was maintained by her own stonelike impenetrability.

After this realization we switched the exaggeration technique to an emphasis on the opposite of her behavior. After reentering the stonelike condition of her arms and hands we began the exercise.

"If you were not stone, what would your arms be like?"

"Light, free quick, open!"

"Do what you said with your arms."

She could not, at this point. The attempt was a compromise between the immobility of her habitual set and the free motion of her fantasy. The patient made a movement with both arms whose significance was inescapable: she was pushing someone away.

This patient, incidentally, did considerable homework with the exaggeration technique. To her own intellectual surprise, she soon reported freer exchanges with her class members, then involvement with her work on a much more intense level of curiosity, and an altogether more pliable, less stonelike, responsiveness to social contacts. Her body work in the sessions reflected the new freedom. She could move her arms in any way she wished, and did so expressively and with pleasure.

We are not implying here that arm gymnastics cause receptive social intercourse. We are describing a focus technique. Its exercise places a focus of attention on the person's area of neglect. What then happens to that neglect depends on more than technical exercises. It depends on the interest of the patient who has now found added freedom of choice.

Not an uncommon case in our society is the patient who has a highly developed foreground attitude of sweetness and light. Predictably, and with no regard for the circumstances, there is always the benign smile, the tolerant patience, the mindless love which no longer communes with anything living but relates only to the purest ideals. Nevertheless, this saint is in therapy.

Once again, here is a case with background qualities that have atrophied or are repressed. Exaggeration technique can get the patient in touch with his neglected aspects. The patient might be asked to try to play-act toughness, anger, or the sort of harsh aggressiveness which has been dramatically amputated out of his customary repertoire. Or instead of this opposite exaggeration, the therapist might mimic utter sweetness. This only, however, if the parody can be managed without hostile sting. It would be precisely the quality which the patient has learned to counter with a good deal of invulnerability. The therapist's act would then only reinforce the patient's prominent quality, which is categorical niceness.

A warning apropos of the devices of those who shine forth sweetly in a rotten world. This stance of lonely goodness can ask for and will often get a cut-rate version of compassion, namely pity. Once the therapist feels sorry for the patient he has been effectively rendered impotent. Pity, which is less than compassion because it is merely an inactive contemplation of somebody else's pain, will make it impossible for the therapist to crack the whip on the patient's stubborn rigidity. To cause pain while feeling sorry automatically means doing harm. Pity the patient, and his character structure remains inviolate. Now the therapist has been converted to the preservation of the patient's status quo, an adroit example of the tyranny of the weak. End of therapy.

There are other examples of predominant, immutable types of behavior and all of them, if the patient is willing, can become malleable again. The techniques we have discussed and also illustrated are designed to help the resistant patient to explore by degrees. In that way he can inject touch and his own life into the habit which has become an impersonal force. All these focusing techniques are a way of looking once again at the dark and forgotten background of the patient's gestalt.

TRANSFERENCE: A SPECIAL CASE OF RESISTANCE

The condition of transference was discovered and described in the context of Freud's development of psychoanalysis. Then and now transference means the patient investing of the therapist with characteristics that are typical of his relationship to his parents and their significant surrogates. The patient sets up a relationship with the therapist in which the patient becomes the son or the daughter and the therapist becomes the father or mother.

Psychoanalytic literature describes well and extensively what transference is, how it occurs, and how it can be dealt with. Very briefly, the therapeutic contribution of the work details how the therapist becomes a good father or a good mother in contrast to the bad parent qualities that have affected the patient. The relevant literature stresses how to promote patient improvement by interpretations which are made at the appropriate times.

None of this is easy, and a thorough knowledge of the pertinent literature is indispensable for every therapist. However, in the context of our existential approach the emphasis of our interest in transference is somewhat different.

In the transference situation the therapist does not become the father. Our thesis is not new, but our stress on the following point is important: what is transferred to the therapist are the patient's attitudes. If a transference relationship is to result, the therapist must then fall into the role which the patient "transfers" upon him. Traditionally, this distortion imposed upon the relationship is encouraged. In our technique we do not encourage it.

The illusion that is built into the transference, the distortion of the existential situation, the resistances which maintain the as-if encounter of the transference situation—we treat these like any other resistance situation, as detailed in the sections of the focus techniques.

Instead of encouraging the sine qua non of psychoanalytic therapy, viz., the transference neurosis, we attempt to break up and dissolve its formation as it occurs in the therapeutic relationship. The reason for our preference for this manner of treatment is implicit in every aspect of this book: something is happening *now;* in order to deal with it, we must know what it is. And the further or the longer the existential condition is an illusion not recognized for what it is, the less we serve the transformation of the patient.

When transference occurs and the involvement is close to being worked out, then something new develops in the relationship between patient and therapist. The distortions of past conditioning drop away and the interpersonal relationship begins to rest on existential grounds. Now the patient no longer sees or treats the therapist as a repository of past experiences, as a fiction, but he responds to the man who sits there with him. In this existential phase of therapy we hear a good phrase very often: "I feel as if I had not really looked at you before—"

Our existential techniques are designed to achieve this phase with better dispatch and with more participation by the patient than seems possible with the historical approach. In practice, transference and existential phases may repeat themselves variously. We mention this as an example not of failure but of work.

In our experience, a great number of contemporary patients come into therapy with no significant transference problems. The therapeutic relationship can begin as an existential one. In such cases a transference neurosis may never develop. We furthermore feel that its occurrence is not a therapeutic necessity and therefore would never encourage its development. Transference is another instance of distortion in a relationship. As it interferes with growth it is a resistance.

The transference relationship maintains itself as long as the patient can project depersonalized pieces of himself onto the therapist. We deal with these projections in the same way we deal with any projection: Through a series of steps the patient must again acknowledge the projection as a rejected aspect of himself, and through that contact experience with his own outcast children he can now deal with them. Their existence as fictions ends at that point. The strength with which they had been invested becomes the patient's own again—to do with as he sees fit, not as his outcast self has seen fit.

We have left a pertinent question to the end, not because we can detail an answer but because it arises persistently: How do we distinguish between affect that is based on transference and affect in a relationship that is grounded existentially?

There is a feel to the difference, a sense of distinction, which will grow with experience. There is a feel of fervor in the ghost-ridden affect which seems to spring from nowhere, which carries you beyond the sense of the present situation, which might surprise you with its presence, and which last but not least obscures in a perceptible way the presence of the person to whom the affect is addressed. That feeling was not generated in this relationship. In contrast, when the affect vitalizes the interest in what is going on now, when it sharpens the dimension and concreteness of the person addressed, when the fervor or the calm of the affect adds to the grip on the ongoing events, then this affect is generated in the existential relationship.

We make this description without any claim to scientific exactitude. We have no language at our command that can do more than gesture at a thing which lives in motion, the feeling of being here or of not being quite here. But with less ambition we can give two helpful guidelines that can distinguish between transference feelings and existential feelings.

If the patient's regard, affect, or feeling for the therapist has no counterpart in the therapist, then we are most likely dealing with an instance of transference.

If the patient is in transference, then he will respond with considerable predictability. In contrast, the patient's feelings for his therapist are bound to be variable and quite clearly responsive to what is going on between the two people in the session.

If the patient displays transference but has gained an existential grip, then he will react *to* the transference.

If he is not with the existential moment, then he will react *in* transference.

But while the patient is climbing in and out of his illusions, what of the therapist?

COUNTERTRANSFERENCE: FEELINGS
OF THE THERAPIST

In the psychoanalytic tradition the feelings of the therapist for the patient are regarded as countertransference.

Just as the patient will project childhood feelings on the therapist, so will the therapist project on the patient from the unfinished business of his own constellations. In that sense, the most adequate therapist would be the one who is relatively free of countertransference. He is at his best when he has no personal feelings for the patient but instead functions as an objective screen, as an affectless observer.

Countertransference does occur. The therapist may project attitudes and feelings on the patient and the resulting distortion effect is no aid in therapy. But we have tried to distinguish between transference affect and existential responsiveness. It is the therapist's responsibility to become sensitive to the distinction, and the refinement of this sense is of course a major goal of supervised training.

However, we do not think that an extirpation of all affect or feeling is a good means of removing the problem of countertransference.

To feel something for the patient implies an involvement and we would go so far as to say that the therapist who is not involved with his patient is no better equipped to do therapy than Pavlov's bell-ringing box.

This involvement does not include giving the patient the therapist's neurosis but it does mean the offer of the sort of personal feeling without which few patients in distress are going to open up. We have given our notion of the therapist at his best: he responds from his center. But the therapist will have various feelings for the patient. . . .

Here is a patient who picks up a favorite statuette from the therapist's desk and smashes the fragile thing against the wall.

It would now take a strangely frozen therapist to show no reaction at all. In point of fact, we think that the therapist will now get very angry. If that is his emotion, then we suggest that he *be* angry. The reaction, to say the least, is an appropriate response to the existential situation and the patient—from one human being to another—would understand the anger better than some display of dead calm.

The therapist may now take his anger and punch the patient in the nose with it, at which point we ask only one question: was this orgy of self-expression consistent with the therapeutic situation or was it an instance in which the therapist used the patient for purposes exclusively his own?

If the therapist uses restraint on the pressure of his emotion—as he might—let it not be in order to fake another emotion or to pretend that there is no reaction at all. Let the true emotion be known. Let its expression remain within the limits of the job at hand: the development—not the use—of the patient.

We would like to emphasize that any blanket assumption that emotion on the part of the therapist in a case of transference removes the event from existential inspection. The therapist's anger at the statue smasher may well have its remote sources in the therapist's infantile power diagram of father-child-mother. However, we feel that the encounter in the session, which is the soil in which growth will occur, is obliterated when ignored for the benefit of a theoretical construct.

It is the therapist's responsibility to stay in touch with the interpersonal encounter of the session. He can lose touch by using the patient for his personal emotive orgy, and he can lose touch by treating a transference diagram instead of an ongoing clash with this one human being. Once feelings occur, they must be made part of the therapeutic situation. And that includes, of course, the event when the therapist's emotional reaction to the patient is truly a countertransference.

We have said that we want to dissolve transference as it occurs and we have suggested the earmarks of a transference feeling in contrast to a feeling that is relevant to the situation. If these earmarks of consistency of emotion and of surprising unrelatedness occur, then the therapist who is now aware of his countertransference can instantly make the event part of the present with which he and the patient must deal. The method is simple in its directness. "I'm sorry,"says the therapist. "This had nothing to do with you. This feeling had nothing to do with anything you have done. I read something into you and lost sight of you for the moment. Let us try and find our way back."

Once again, confusion over the here-and-now has been kept out of the relationship.

ABOUT PHYSICALLY TOUCHING THE PATIENT

We have, in effect been speaking of expressive behavior in the therapeutic relationship. We have suggested that we are expressive, so as not to
hide what is there, and we have urged that the manner of expression be
governed by one overriding consideration only: does it brighten the therapeutic encounter, or does it muddle it?

The orientation pertains whether the therapist gets angry at a statue
smasher, whether he feels affectionate toward a patient who cries out of his
loneliness, or, as a matter of fact, whether the therapist feels sexual attrac-
tion.

When it exists it is there and when it is there, deal with it. In addition
to all we have said about the matter of maintaining the therapeutic encounter, we need say only one thing about the economics of sexual feelings between patient and therapist: As a sexual object the patient ceases to be patient and the therapist, *mutatis mutandis*, stops being therapist. The con-
suming concentration of the sexual encounter obviates any considerations
but those which serve that particular partnership, with its physical power,
and with its own personal merging. Sex may be therapeutic, but it is not
therapy.

But in this connection, a note about the matter of touching the patient. We mention the topic because there is a tacit taboo about touching
for many therapists. We mention touching also because of its power as
a therapeutic tool.

The convention of avoiding physical contact with the patient has the
same rationale as the old dictum which says that the therapist should avoid
social contact with the patient. In both cases, the existential encounter
interferes with the transference situation. The illusion upon which classical
therapy wants to focus its work is apt to be dissipated. Since that dissipation
is precisely the object of our work, we have nothing against touching the
patient. When physical touching can enhance the patient's existential
awareness, we recommend touch.

It is almost impossible to conceptualize a physical touch. For that
reason, the skin contact may be precisely the aid which can reorient the
patient toward a type of awareness which has been canceled out by conceptual concentration.

For example, a young male patient whose barriers to emotional
awareness were a major problem gained a great deal from repeated, very
simple encounters such as these:

"How do you feel?" asked the therapist at a point when the
patient was grinning brightly while describing the shambles of his recent
love affair.

"Fine," said the patient.

"I don't feel that this one word sums it up very well," said the therapist.

"Of course not." And now the young man hitched around in his seat for a square view at the therapist and a level-headed account of his chaotic love situation. The tape of his delivery records the patient's characteristic mode of experience: "I am faced with someone else's impulsive act, I would call it, and the consequences of that behavior, of that irresponsibility, shall we say, are the very things, the flotsam and jetsam, so to speak, which I now see floating by. There is undoubtedly something salvageable in all that mess, however, for the moment, in view of that mess, I must take my time inspecting instead of plunging in there once again."

"How do you feel about that??"

"I have a considerable amount of reorienting to do. I feel that to be true."

At this point the therapist decided that the patient had missed the point long enough. The intellectual response, the device of noninvolvement, these were precisely the limitations of the patient's experiential capacity.

"I don't think," said the therapist, "that you understand what I mean by *feel*. Let me show you what I mean. Close your eyes, please."

When the patient had closed his eyes the therapist reached over and put his hand over the patient's hand.

"What do you feel?"

"You've reached over, " said the patient.

"That is an intelligent conclusion. That is *not* what you *feel*."

"Oh. You mean on my hand?"

"What do you feel?"

"I feel that you are touching my hand in order to make sort of a demonstration."

"Another conclusion," said the therapist. Try and forget about your explanations for the moment and simply tell me what you feel in your hand."

"Oh. I feel your hand."

"Stay with it, please."

"Okay. I'm not moving."

"I know. But are you feeling my hand?"

"Sure." However, as a matter of record, it took the better part of the session until this young patient abandoned his speculations about why he was being touched, what the purpose of the "demonstration" might be, and before he ceased short-circuiting any raw sensation by conceptualizing it out of existence.

Then he said, "I feel your hand."

"No you don't," said the therapist.

"But I do! I feel the pressure and the warmth."

"Finally," said the therapist. "Now please stay on that feeling level and tell me what your hand feels."

In this instance, the patient was able to verbalize why he did not feel. "I kept busting it up with thoughts. That's when I can't feel a thing—"

Aside from a general desensitization problem, as in the case of the young man who gradually learned the difference between thinking and feeling, there are frequent instances of particular body desensitizations which have a dynamic relationship to the patient's conflict situation. There is the dead feeling in the hands, which will not grip; the absence of feeling around the eyes, which stare stiffly without seeing; the anaesthesia in the shoulders which are hunched in chronic readiness to deliver a violent punch with the fist. These are only some examples of desensitizations which are soon discovered when therapy includes the instructions to range with feeling about the entire body image. Very frequently, the therapist will learn to observe the characteristics of stance or absence of motion which marks the desensitized area. Then touch, in one form or another, can help reestablish contact for the patient with the active repression involved.

Sometimes the patient can be asked to massage the dead area and to report the change or the return of feeling. More often we have found it best for a start when the therapist does the massaging, because the patient will try to avoid dislodging the desensitization when he touches himself.

We have inadvertently found in this connection that there is often something very revealing—like a new discovery—for the patient who receives a touch that is not exploitative. In our culture, or at least in our patient population, there tends to be a prevalent expectation that to be touched means to have something taken away. (The vernacular reflects this expectation: to "touch" sombody for a loan.) The unexploitative touch is a good discovery. We are here reminded of the meaning and function of the laying on of hands. In that case, which is unexploitative touching, something is given. (Once again, there is a vernacular use of this meaning: to lay something on a person is hippie slang for giving that person something.)

And so we find that there is no taboo about physically touching in therapy anyway. Physical touch can begin to reawaken the absence of knowing that keeps a resistance intact, and physical touch can open the road so often obscured by our thick growth of intellectual constructs, the road toward living with feeling again.

PROJECTION: THE TARGET FOR EVERY TECHNIQUE

We have described the focusing techniques and some of their objects of attention. The techniques, as described, can be used to work on single—if not simple—feelings which we want to bring back into the full concert of the patient's experience. We have gone through the fog or scaled the wall or melted the ice which was the resistance and have found the hidden experience of grief, hate, love, anger, fright.

But the split-off portions of the personality may have found a much more complicated sanctuary which, like a systematic labyrinth, guards our patient's minotaur.

Resistances may stand out singly. They stand out not because they are alone but simply because they are the most prominent modes in which the patient communicates to us his own life situation. This foreground of resistances is usually a part of that patient's unique and interwoven net of background resistances which altogether make up his present mode of living in the world. They support each other. They form his resistance complex.

This web, more often than not serves to provide the well-secured setting for the crown jewel of the resistance complex, the projection system.

The utility of projections are well known both in practice and in the literature. They rid us of unwanted aspects of our personality. They justify expression of our forbidden emotions because the same have been projected onto others and now our own use of them is justified under the assault of our fabricated reality. Our gain in temporary safety through projection is paid for by a constant drain on our energy required to maintain the projection. The system tends to be self-reinforcing, a maintenance for which we pay by a constant drain on our energy required to maintain the projection. The system tends to be self-reinforcing, a maintenance for which we pay by ever more frugal self-limitations in being alive in this world. We have nothing to add to this Torah for the sustenance of our self-made ghosts. We add this section only to suggest a progression of steps which can make inviolate projections accessible to dissolution. This is done by their creator, the patient, who can drain them of their power by once again taking his own back into himself.

Work with simple projections requires no more than a brief word. They are confronted as images and therefore the recommended steps are those of the image technique. In the case of more complex projections we recommend a series of developmental steps which progressively acquaint the patient with his projection, which allow him to identify its qualities as his own, and which then make a choice of their use once again possible. The successive steps are concrete: *First,* ask for detailed description of the projection. *Second,* encourage the patient to act as if he were the projection. *Third,* intensify the game of imagination by asking the patient to speak of the projection entirely in the first person. *Fourth,* engage in confrontive discourse with the patient *as* the first-person projection. During the progress of the last step the patient is most apt to accept the realization that he is no longer playing a game, that the projection is in fact an aspect of himself. The *fifth* and last step of this schema is the work done with the reabsorbed feelings. Since they are at this point the patient's own again, therapeutic work is most identical to the therapeutic work we do with any other feelings.

For purposes of illustration we shall describe the complex projections as two in kind. Then we will give tape excerpts that demonstrate work done with these types by using the progressive steps of our five-step schema. One type of complex projection is the imagery of characterological representations. These are characters of pure invention such as witches, policemen, beasts, strange or common people of many descriptions—but they are usually inventions rather than real people whom the patient knows. The second type of projection which is in accessible form for work with the schema does not consist of objects. They are not projections as such but rather the known, resultant feeling with which the patient is left when he projects. Examples are characteristic fears in typical situations or habitual emotions which arise in inappropriate and bothersome context. Our tape excerpts should help illustrate these general descriptions.

In stepwise fashion, here is the work that was done with a 40-year-old patient, an artist, whose projection took the form of a despicable Prussian officer. The dominant and nagging complaint of this patient was his personal worthlessness, the shallowness of his work which was commercial rather than artistic, the rootlessness of his existence, which was demonstrated to him in the many moves he had made and in the fact of the geographic dispersion of his family. In the context of feeling in "slovenly despair" one day, he described a projection which he had begun to admire for its qualities of contrast: A Prussian army officer. A resolute, well-uniformed man who knew what was right and what was wrong, who came from a well-organized family background, who had an acknowledged place in his world, and who never had to worry about who he was.

"Describe him."

"I just did. You mean the man himself?"

"Yes. Look at him and tell me what he is like."

"He is strong. He walks with a sharp, certain step."

"What is he doing?"

"He is returning the salute of an enlisted man."

"How?"

"Just a minute—he's turning around and calling the sergeant back."

Under prompting, the patient began to invent a dialogue between officer and enlisted man. This sequence, it should be mentioned, did not occur until the third time that the patient had used this projection during a session. In other words, he had by now acquainted himself with the imaginary officer a good deal.

In terms of our schema, the mere descriptions of the projection were completed at this point. We now encouraged the second step of the schema in which the patient acts like the projection.

"He says," the patient reported about his officer image, "that the sergeant should come back and try that salute over, God damn it, and not so sloppy this time."

"That didn't sound very convincing," said the therapist. "Try to sound like the officer."

The patient tried with some embarrassment. But with gentle encouragement, which included some mimicking by the therapist in this case, the patient got into the spirit of the game. Enacting the officer, the patient's voice became harsh and severe. The content of the reprimand became punitive. But then the patient showed that he was getting disturbed. He glanced anxiously at the therapist a few times and his officer monologue became flat.

"Would you like to stop?" asked the therapist.

"Yes." The patient sat back with a sigh.

"Are you back in the room now?"

"Thank God, yes."

After a pause for lighting a cigarette the therapist then tried to make the projection work somewhat more accessible to the patient.

"Do you remember the voice you used?"

"God yes. I can still hear it ringing in my ears. He's some vicious—*attrappe*."

"I don't know the word."

"A faker! All that vicious show of force to fake away just how hollow he is inside that uniform!"

"Did you hear your voice just now?"

"Never mind my voice! I *hate* that bastard!"

The therapist did not pursue the projection work at this point. In his judgment, the patient was too revolted with the projection to reengage in step two, which was to act as if he were the projection. By the same token, step three, in which the patient acts his projection out in the first person, was quite out of the question.

Step three, as a matter of fact, was not possible for several sessions. Then the patient introduced the next step himself.

"If I were that Prussian," he said, "I'd have a hell of a time living with myself."

"Not the way you've described him in the past. He seemed so controlled."

"Hah!"

"Can you show me?"

"Show you what?"

"This time," said the therapist, "let's try exploring the officer from the inside. Imagine you are he."

"I don't want to."

"I know."

But this time the patient was ready. He smiled at the therapist and got an encouraging smile in return. He then talked with the now familiar hard ring in his voice, his posture stiffened, and he looked at the therapist with disdain.

"I am the same as before. I don't change. That is my strength. That permanence, that eternal—forever—unending—"

The emphasis of stiff strength continued for a while longer until the patient interrupted, visibly exhausted.

"Did you feel your strength?" asked the therapist.

"*My* strength?" The reaction was so incredulous that the therapist did not press the point, for fear of eliciting a sharp rejection of the reabsorption process. As a case in point, the patient remained in an all too typical fashion at this close but incomplete point of reaccepting his projection for over a month.

At this point of the work we know of no technique. We only know that it is hard work, over and over. However, now our third phase is feasible, in which the therapist engages in discourse with the patient *as* the projection. Excerpts of this work toward the end run as follows.

"I would not deny the strength," said the therapist. "I look at you and I can palpably feel it."

"What you feel and what I feel is not the same thing," said the patient-as-officer.

"Then show me more clearly what I don't see."

"All you see is the uniform."

"Yes. I see that too."

"And the strength, undoubtedly because of the stiff neck, the hard chest, all that."

"Yes. Now tell me how you feel."

"I feel—exhausted inside."

"You, the Prussian officer?"

"Yes."

And at long last, the projection became knowingly absorbed.

"Yes," said the patient and resumed his own posture again. "I am he."

"He is some of you, as I see you."

"I have that strength, you know that? I have it, I misuse it, as he does, and so I exhaust myself—"

At this point, work on the patient's feelings, not the Prussian officer's feelings, began.

At this point the patient knows, of course, what this is all about. And yet he will nevertheless attempt to project again, he will belittle the progress as foolish play-acting, and he will despair in the use of his reabsorbed strength and attempt to toss it away.

Again, there are no therapeutic tricks in this work, but only work. It is necessary for patient and therapist to simply stick it out in paced rhythms of forward as well as backward steps.

But we do not let him forget his gains, that sense of reabsorbed strength, that loss of the ghost-ridden life, and even the comfort of honest exhaustion. . . .

We promised a second example of work with projections, in which the patient does not present a complex image with a life of its own, but rather complains in effect about the depletion effect which his projection has given him. This example will not take as long as the first, because all we need to detail are the steps by means of which we help the patient define a projection and then the five schematized steps we have described follow in their needed order.

We had a patient whose abiding complaint was a crushing sense of embarrassment whenever his work required him to confront a group. He was an architect of considerable accomplishment and would have been content to create his work in the solitude of his studio. However, the plans, proposals, and the complicated financing of his large-scale work forced him continuously into conferences with many people. We commenced work on the unknown projections by asking for a detailed description of one of those embarrassment situations. The patient picked a vivid one. As it turned out, embarrassment did not describe his state. He had been terrified.

The following steps took a number of sessions but the abbreviated rendition shows the actual sequence of events.

"Describe the meeting to me in detail."

"I just couldn't look at anybody. I forgot my points, the points I had to make, I just stood there."

"We will both see this more clearly by being there," said the therapist. "Imagine you are there."

"Please—"

"It's a game, if you like. Play it that way, and then we'll see what goes on."

After a number of slip-and-slide tries to get into and out of the situation of the meeting, the patient succeeded in facing the situation once again, while in session. He repeated the sensations of his terror.

"What terrifies you most? What's the worst they can do to you?"

"Make a fool of me."

"How?"

"Semmerling can. The banker. He can say that the whole proposal is put that way to make money only, and not, like I said, to save money."

The patient's power projection was at this point clear to the therapist, namely that the patient felt defenseless in front of the group because he had given the power of ridicule to the figure of old Semmerling.

A short-cut attempt to regain the projected strength was in this case partly successful. The patient was asked if there was anything that might embarrass old Semmerling. Details aside, there was. Then the patient was encouraged to experience in the session his own power to ridicule anyone in his audience. With some work on his rejected ability to embarrass the group he might face, his symptom of embarrassment vanished.

We mention the case as an instance of an efficiency move which worked well enough to improve the patient's specific work situations. However, the patient wished to continue his sessions. He was not totally free of concern over his symptom and he was distantly but persistently concerned over his newly discovered talent for ridiculing other people. The patient reintroduced the figure of old Semmerling and therapy then continued toward a deeper solution by the use of the projection-dissolving steps detailed in the previous example.

We would like to add that the byways through which old Semmerling had reappeared turned out to be an example of the projection's reinforcing quality. This is the self-fulfilling prophecy.

With an equal proportion of will and doubt the patient had tackled Semmerling for a test run of power. Confronting the older man, our patient had attempted to try a real-life maneuver of embarrassing Semmerling. But the attempt had been half-hearted and, in effect, strictly ridiculous. Semmerling, of course, was just the man to tell our patient so. In this way, the patient had acted precisely the role for which his power projection on Semmerling had prepared him: on the one hand the expectation of being ridiculed, and on the other, the very behavior that would invite the expected treatment.

This reinforcing quality of projections, this device of the self-fulfilling prophecy, is possibly the most powerful agent in the function of projection systems which keeps the conjuring force of the curse alive. It is this aspect of projections which speaks to the cognitive aspect of our personality. We remain fixed by the mesmeric eye of this ghost and increasingly sharpen our talents by logic, test, and proof. Our intellect leaps in hyperlife under the stare of projections, while the rest of us sickens and floats off into pseudolife.

You see it—but the victim does not. The sickening confines of the victim's existence can wrench the heart, but the man who is victimized by his projections does not even realize his disaster! It is at such a point of superior knowledge and of clearer understanding that we may well be fired into rescue action. Which brings us to the last of the techniques to be mentioned.

THE MORALITY TECHNIQUE · MANIPULATION

This technique is not psychotherapy.

Any psychotherapeutic encounter, regardless of school or technique, has one basic aim: that the patient may change. All the techniques we have mentioned have this process of change as their goal: to help the patient find his way—to free him so that he can make a choice. The way is his own and the choice is his. Anything less is not therapy, and anything more is manipulation.

But here is the technique that tells the patient how he should be. Manipulation is the active arm of the takeover syndrome, the state that describes the imposition of standards, goals, ideals, dogmas, and all the eternal truths that have been invented for the purpose of making choice unnecessary and of perpetuating the fiction of certainty in our lives.

Certainty should be, but uncertainty *is.* Those who cannot bear this do not enter therapy but enter the army, or any number of other states of dependence that relieve them of the burdens of being unique and alone—which is to say, an individual.

As for the manipulator, it does not matter to our description of the takeover syndrome whether he wishes to act for or against the object of his manipulations. He affects change without the active participation of the individual for whom he cares. And that includes a sufficient application of superior knowledge or force to counter opposition to manipulatory change. We have now described coercion.

Psychologically speaking, the naïvest form of coercion is preaching, the cleverest form is the art of propaganda, and the most insidious form is the new art of brainwashing. In every instance, the manipulator takes over for the individual under his care. Success of the takeover syndrome is in every case measured by increased proximity to an extrapersonal ideal, at the price of a reduction in individuality.

While the scope and effectiveness of a Hitler may be a far cry from the manipulative influence of a well-meaning therapist, the comparison stands because of the quality of coercion.

It is true, in a manner of speaking, that we too have an ideal, and it is explicitly stated: To give therapy when asked; to give the strength to bear doubt on one's own; to be able to allow the other to be in a choice of his own.

This is the meaning of being at center: to know what is there and to allow it to be. Then to care for another cannot become an act of imposition, but it can at its best become an act of love. To give without the purpose of obtaining a rewarding effect, when the giving act is its own satisfaction; then we feel, we learn of love.

chapter 5

The Emerging Personality

THE PATIENT FINDS HIS CENTER

Now that the patient emerges from the harsh struggles of the character work he begins to change in striking and in unpredictable ways. All the effort of therapy so far has been the groundwork which now makes the emergence of his own existential phase possible. The characteristic descriptions of a particular patient no longer fit.

Predictability of behavior depends upon the degree of sameness, the rigidity of habit, with which the patient makes encounters in his life. Now the old suit has split in the seams and is dropping away. The live body is starting to show.

Projections and neurotic attachments are falling away. The distortions which the patient has imposed on his world are replaced by a singular directness of contact with the things about him. He achieves an awareness of what is there. This awareness is a function of a new achievement: the patient can let be what is there. This awareness can be contemplative or it can be curious in its absorption with what is being seen, but its chief characteristic is the new ability to allow a phenomenon to unfold itself. There is no longer the need or habitual necessity to instantly take over an event, to change it, to control it, to make it a possession or to make it predictable. The patient's newfound sense of self-possession makes all that unnecessary. As we have said, he can let things be and he can permit them their own rhythms of change and evolvement.

The neurotic necessity to control is lessening. The compulsion to instantly manipulate the environment into an invention of one's own design is no longer built into the behavior. And once again we have described the state of being at center.

In the context of our own cultural emphasis on particular kinds of action, the description of being at center tends to sound like a state of passivity. We point out, however, that an absence of a need to control is precisely posited on the condition of being in remarkable self-possession of one's available strength. The man at center does not question his capacities. Therefore he does not have to test them. Therefore the use of his strength is confidently available to him, as he sees fit. This sense of self may not be demonstrative, but it is no more passive than it is action-bent. When at center, the plus and minus signs of *do* or *don't*, *take* or *don't take it*, *yes* or *no*, *should* or *shouldn't* are simply meaningless. That is why we have spoken of the state at center as being without value judgments, without prescriptions for assessing and controlling an event as it unfolds itself independently of the observer.

The state at center is an active state simply because it maintains itself. We think of the still image of the fish suspended in the medium of his world—and there is the image of being at one's center by virtue of a balanced exchange of unifying motions. The man at his center is no more shut off from the world than the fish that is alert to every current of his world for the sake of his harmony and his balance.

Now when at center the patient for the first time becomes aware of the life and rhythms which are not of his own making. He recognizes otherness precisely when he begins to respond, to flow, we would call it, with the rhythms around him. Only now is he truly responsive. It sounds paradoxical in our language, but now we can say that being one with the world can occur only when being one with one's self, and that being fully one's self makes a full sense of belonging in the world possible.

And so we have described how the patient, as individual, becomes aware of the other rhythms around him because he can flow with them now. This is good contact. This is impersonal empathy.

This state of awareness which amounts to a flowing with the rhythms of the other phenomenon, this particular nonjudging sensitivity, becomes now critically important for the work of the therapist. The patient has dissolved basic resistances. Only now is he able to make discoveries about himself. And this is what he begins to do now, unpredictably, in novel ways, and with a good deal of experimental verve. The therapist's attending, as described, was never as important as now. The closer the emergent patient comes to his center, the more willing is he to take risks!

HOW THE PATIENT PERCEIVES CHANGE IN HIMSELF

The success of character work is felt by the patient in two general ways. The more objective change is symptom relief, the more subjective development is a sense of peace and of freedom. From the point of view of the theoretically oriented therapist the much more significant alterations in the patient may be such matters as renewed availability of energy which is no longer bound up in resistance or reductions in anxiety with concomitant decrease in the rigidity of various mechanisms of defense. These explanatory constructs are not patient criteria of improvement. If they are, the patient is probably not feeling a thing. But he knows when his symptoms have disappeared. If the presenting complaint was insomnia and if blessed sleep now comes again, then the patient knows that he has improved. The economy of his neurosis may at the same time demand night sweats which appear like an alternate symptomatic expression to the symptom that has been abandoned, but if the patient does not mind nights sweats as much as insomnia, then we would feel he has improved. From our therapeutic point of view we too would view this symptom change as a sign of improvement, though perhaps not for the same reason as the patient does. For us, the patient has made progress because he displays more flexibility than before, if only in the choice of his symptomatology.

But the more significant report of improvement which the patient describes toward the end of character work is much more subjective than symptom loss. It also reflects much vaster (or deeper) personality alterations.

"I told you which way I come here everytime," said a patient. "Today, just like that, I took the long way along the river road instead."

Objectively, the patient's change in route was a minor alteration in behavior. But subjectively, his sense of bright-eyed and adventuresome happiness reflected a vast loosening of rigidity in his make-up.

"I haven't told you before," said another, "but I've been shaving in the same succession of steps for I don't know how many years. For a while now I've shaved in a different way just about every day; neck, cheeks, chin, upper lip—all in different order."

His experience that more choice is available to him may be vague, but also much more encompassing.

"I walked into my office today, past Ann's desk, and so help me I saw Ann sitting there, not Ann the secretary but this woman called Ann, and that for the first time since I don't know when! And when we smiled at each other, so help me, that was new too!"

The function of neurosis is to make safe by constriction of consciousness and through invariability of behavior. We now witness a broadening and flexing of both. Some patients simply report an increased sense of feeling free, of feeling less crowded by objects and events in their environment. They speak of fewer demands made upon them by life. This is equivalent to saying that demands are met more easily and thereby, of course, a demand ceases to exist.

The patient now finds himself more unique. The danger of standing out and of being different is no longer such a matter of concern. He likes who he is, he becomes his own friend again. It is at this point that we observe the patient who begins to place such a high premium on his uniqueness that being different may become a neurotic orientation itself. The conformist lives by "should." The nonconformist lives by "should not." Neither is freed for choice and this leap from the frying pan into the fire is a not uncommon adventure which the patient commits toward the end of his therapy.

For us the most noteworthy event at this point of therapy is the apperance of a new kind of panic.

"I am at home, sitting at peace," reported one patient, "and I am really experiencing this novel thing, this ability to sit in silence. There is none of that push, pull, strain, restrain struggle that's been going on inside all the time. I'm calm and look around—and then suddenly, out of nowhere—I take that back—out of me there leaps this absolute fright! *What if I lose this again?!* What if I can't find this good sense of harmony ever again?"

The patient who has found his center has found a great deal. Now he can lose a great deal. That is the novel panic.

We would like to point out a differential characteristic concerning the loss of center. It was well verbalized by a patient who expressed the entirely different experience of moving away from his center in one case, and of "losing" it in the other.

"I noticed getting away from my center, as you call it, at the office. I'm sitting there and know I'm not in that quiet seeing state. I'm busy and haven't got time for that mountain-top serenity. The rushes have to get out, Stage Three isn't ready, wardrobe wants to know if they could use the Civil War uniforms for the crowd scene where Napoleon gets deported, and then—did I tell you?—that dumb diva's doctor calls up and says she isn't getting fat but she's sure getting pregnant. So to hell with the center. I'm a producer and I got to produce. I'm not worried."

In effect, the patient has here described not so much any involuntary loss of center, but a move from center to periphery as a perfectly appropriate answer to the demands of his activity. An environmental demand has been met. But now he continues to describe a contrasting experience.

"Now there's no reason for all that *kakamakie* of do this, do that and get every *schlemiel* on the job in time. I'm just standing there by the truck, under the boom, and watch them do the scene, and good too. They're doing their job and I'm just standing there, taking it all in. Center again. And right then and there something takes a leap in me, a scream wants to leap out, screaming: I've lost it, what happened? I tell you what happened. *I interfered with me.* I pushed my fine state of being out of the way and pushed me, the shivering, nervous Napoleon type back into place. I lost it, that other way, that open way, because I shut the door on it!"

This tape about the center state and the loss of it is one which reflects many observations of a similar kind. There is, at this point in therapy, a typical apprehension, if not fear, over losing the newly found openness to the world, the state of self-possession. There is once again the fear of getting trapped in the net of tensions which have chronically interfered with living a receptive and a responsive life. As the insight of the last patient demonstrates, there is a world of a difference between not using the center and of losing it. The former is a move away from the center by choice. The latter is a move away from the center by the reactivation of the automatic defenses which character work has not fully dissolved.

There is one more experience of change which the patient typically discovers toward the end of the character work. So far his preoccupations and his encounters have been with himself. Now his vision moves further. Now he encounters people. He has become able to explore his relationships and he will actively do so. He makes new discoveries about his familiar ties. For example, his spouse or his children become the source of fresh love—or of sudden frictions. And, quite predictably, he will now look at his therapist as a person with whom he has developed human ties. Opening himself as he does, the patient becomes aware not only of new excitement but also of risk.

THE LIGHT TOUCH

We have moved close now to termination, and once again there occurs one of those critical points in the phases of therapeutic work where small neglects on the part of the therapist may have disproportionate consequences. The patient has literally become more defenseless, using the term in the sense of the patterned resort to habitual mechanisms of defense. Instead of relying upon visor, breastplate, and mailed fist, he now uses his living muscle. Having found his center, he is open, and any need for defense is now met only with the agility and the variation of his entire psychic structure. The risk of encounter is new and there is once again the temptation to resort to abandoned habits. But we will say this: We have never yet seen the patient who at this point of completion in his character work ever became sicker than he has been before. Yet we want to promise him more. We now help him by using the light, delicate touch.

We speak here of an aspect in the work of the therapist which is equal to an art. Think of the painter. As his senses flow with the making of his work on the canvas the organic demands of his creative act may require for the work of completion one single, bold stroke or the lightest, finest touch. He knows which is appropriate because he attends to his task, he flows with its making. And so must be the attuning of the therapist at this close point to completion.

More than ever before, the patient now sets the pace and we flow with the pace in complementary fashion. Do not bomb him with insights or explanations in order to coerce him into a change. This is his time to experiment with the discovery of new skills.

We now want our touch to be light enough to allow the patient's own movement, but firm enough to be felt.

Tenderness and sympathetic silence may allow an unfolding in the patient. Or it might keep him asleep. Then what is the light touch we wish to practice? It is the delicacy of staying in contact with the other without breaking his rhythm, but knowing what his rhythm is. That is what we respond to—his rhythm. That is what we show him with our response, if the knowledge of his own rhythm has escaped him. The therapist is far less apt to go wrong with observation at this point than with interpretation. The novitiate notion of getting right down to business and to handle the issues at hand in the session is part of the takeover syndrome. The patient must move and grow at his own rate. If he does not, then the growth is not his own. That is the special problem of this stage in therapy.

Here is a part of a tape that shows how the therapist bombed the patient right back into the confines of his armor plating against contact with another human being. This young woman had begun to explore the therapist.

"I felt like stopping at the market on the way over to buy you something."

"I think that was nice. Did you?"

"Yes. I brought you these eggs."

"Thank you. I like that."

"How do you like eggs? I mean, for breakfast, for example."

"Do you know why you are asking me that?"

At this point the patient looked briefly startled. Her personal contact and exploration had been interrupted with a switch in the direction toward topic discussion and away from the personal encounter which she had begun to try out. She gave a theoretical answer about motivations and did not attempt a here-and-now encounter again for an entire, wasted month.

The therapist did not flow with the patient but imposed a direction.

But there is another end to the spectrum of flowing with the other, where the touch of impersonal empathy becomes, *mutatis mutandis*, an alliance with the patient against a common enemy.

It is characteristic in this phase of therapy for the patient to introduce problem encounters with the spouse. Out of numerous examples we cite one.

"He gets drunk every night starting at eight o'clock and I don't like that anymore," said a young woman patient about her husband.

"Since when?"

"I don't know. But I didn't get upset about it before. Now I don't like it. He ignores me, he doesn't make love to me like we used to—I mean, he makes love to me sometimes, yes, but not often enough and not really *with* me. He just uses my body."

"Can you tell him that?"

"Sure. But what's the use? He says that liquor costs less than my therapy and if he could afford therapy the way he's been paying for mine—well, you can see it's useless."

"Yes," said the therapist, and at this point had blundered into the trap. He had adopted the patient's enemy as his own. He had taken sides. He had totally overlooked the essential feature of his task in behalf of the patient, namely the job of helping the patient to find and accept personal responsibility.

"I can understand how he cramps you," was the way in which the therapist recovered in the next session. "He ignores you. He berates you. Now tell me, what is it in you that finds satisfaction with such a person? How did you pick him in the first place?"

The focus was now back on the patient instead of on an enemy who was imputed to be responsible for everything that was going wrong. And since the conflict was between the young woman patient and her husband and not between the therapist and the husband, it was now the proper time for a joint session.

THE JOINT SESSION

The joint session is only necessary when the patient perceives the partner of love or of attachment as the enemy. We warn against seeing the partner alone. This is equivalent to conferring with the enemy behind the victim's back. We urge instead that patient and partner come to the regular session together. Now the distortions of second-hand report and the techniques of blaming can be opened for demonstrable display.

But the therapist does not take sides.

It is the job of the therapist in the joint session to create one thing only: awareness of what one partner is doing to the other. That is the sole aim and purpose of the confrontation between partners in the presence of the therapist.

"You are two people who interact with each other. And you are important to each other. Now we want to see what it is that you do to each other."

This introduced the first session between a male patient and his wife whom the therapist had only known through the reports of the patient. The patient's view of his role in the relationship can be summarized as passive, subjugated, and bullied. His wife was excessively demanding of his time and activities and she enforced her demands with impersonal coolness and an unbending will. The joint session of Mr. Milquetoast and his keeper revealed quite something else.

The wife was stiff, cool, and impersonal while the husband surprised by a consistent technique of bullying and baiting his wife. He domineered her responses at every available point.

Halfway through the session the patient left the room in order to make a phone call. There was an instantly noticeable change in the wife. She physically relaxed and managed a shy smile at the therapist.

"What happened to you?" asked the therapist.

"He terrifies me."

Here was the other side of the view. The cool, reserved woman who had adopted this stance because she was afraid of her husband. When he returned to the room his wife's posture stiffened automatically.

The therapist now introduced this aspect of the relationship into the encounter between husband and wife.

"Did you ever tell him what you just told me?" he asked the wife.

"No."

"What did she say?" asked the husband.

"Look at her and tell me what you see."

The husband looked and said that she sat there withdrawn and rigid.

"Is that what you are doing?" asked the therapist of the wife.

"Yes. That's how it feels."

"Did you ever ask her why she sits that way and acts that way?"

"No. It's just her way."

"Why don't you ask her?"

"Because I know—alright, why?"

"Because I'm afraid of you!" the wife burst out and then broke into tears.

The husband's shock and surprise was dramatic, and this first time encounter opened the way to his recognition of his own, totally overlooked aggressiveness.

We have found it helpful in general for the spouse of a patient to come to the therapy hour every twenty sessions or so. The therapist as observer does not participate in the encounter between patient and spouse as such. That encounter is theirs. But the therapist participates in the action of each partner. "What are you doing now in this response you have made? What is your part, your contribution, in the relationship?"

That is the therapist's part in the joint session. He works to show what each of the partners is doing to the other.

Sometimes, as it turns out, the therapist in his relationship to the patient, may need that same outside view.

MULTIPLE SESSIONS

Sometimes there is the event of the therapeutic impasse. This means that the sessions have gone on but nothing else seems to be going on. The patient is not progressing. The therapist is confused. There is fog in the interaction and there is boredom in the increasingly automatic events. Simply put, the patient has stopped growing and the therapist does not know why. It is at this point that a second therapist may serve well as the therapist to the relationship between the stumped therapist and his stationary patient.

We introduce recognition of the impasse in a direct way to the patient. "It seems to me that things are not going well between us at this moment. I don't understand what is going on. I would like to ask a colleague to join us in a session. Perhaps he can clarify things for us."

There may be resistance to the idea, in which case we discuss the resistance. A patient almost never rejects the idea of a multiple session completely.

The multiple therapist now functions in exactly the same manner as the therapist in the joint session. He is not an external diagnostician but a participant with each of the others.

There are a few warnings. They need only be named. The original therapist may try to enlist the aid of the multiple therapist's support, which amounts to a move against the patient. If such a seduction occurs the multiple therapist must instantly nip that maneuver: "I won't join you in battle against the patient. What is your battle?"

Please note that the multiple session is not therapy supervision, a form of work which can easily be done by simply going over the tape of a session. The multiple therapist is a participant to an interaction whose lines of force need to be worked out. Supervision transacts between two therapists. Multiple-session work transacts between multiple therapist and the patient on one hand, and between multiple and original therapist right then and there in the presence of the patient.

The patient, in that case, has here an opportunity to view a healthy interpersonal relationship. Sometimes, we have found, he may not accept it as such but will attempt to use it in accordance with his life-style of manipulation. In that case the multiple session develops the technique of wedging.

The patient who wedges attempts to play one therapist against the other. This is an attempt to sabotage his own therapy, to stall the flow of growth once again, to perpetuate the stalemate which brought the multiple session into being in the first place. The patient, in the wedging maneuver, will typically ask to see one of the therapists alone. Both tone and intent of the request make clear that the patient wants to belittle the competence of one of the therapists, usually his own. If the original therapist lacks self-support he may easily develop resentment toward his patient at this point. It is therefore essential that the original and the multiple therapist have an open, communicative relationship, so that the topic of personal competence can be freely discussed.

The therapist must be a growing person himself. The rate of growth is the same rate at which the need for multiple sessions diminishes. And ultimately the rate of his growth has the therapeutic effect which makes his patient need him less and less.

ABOUT MOVEMENT AND CHANGE

How permanent is the change that occurs in therapy? Will the changes that occur in psychotherapy persist throughout life?

We don't know. But we know a great deal of the essential unpredictability of anyone's life situation. Therefore if the person's modes of encounter do not change as he grows through his life, then psychotherapy has not been a help to him. The only change which we want to effect in the exercise of psychotherapy is the ability to be able to change. We are sometimes interested in the therapeutic alteration of a specific complaint, the removal of a particular problem situation in the life of a patient. More often, the therapeutic aim is more pervasive and seemingly nonspecific. We want the patient to have his senses back, his feelings, and his muscle. We want him to have all of himself available once again, so that he can advance or retreat by his choice alone. This strength to commit a choice is then equivalent to a responsible act. When he is in command of his faculties, then he is capable of responsibility. We can finish in therapy the unfinished business from the past. We cannot finish the business which has not yet occurred. But the patient, whole again, can go out and do his best.

But the statement "I know myself" is never complete. The work of becoming is the work of being alive. I cannot decide to take a deep breath and inhale once and for all. Instead, there is the rhythm of breath, the rhythm of waking and sleeping, the rhythm of feelings that come forward and retreat. There is a pervasive life rhythm of opposites which the Chinese have formalized in the notion of Yin and Yang. The swing from the light on one to the dark of the other, from the cold of the one to the warmth of the other, that oscillation is the self-renewing rhythm of being alive. A geometric curve can only approximate the experience. An intellectual concept, by virtue of its focus, must make stationary even the concept of motion. There are realities beyond the limits of the intellect. The Koans are ancient ways of impressing this realization upon the Zen student: What is the sound of one hand clapping?

The Zen student, after years of pondering the answer, comes back to his master and delivers his solution. For those intellectual panegyrics he then receives a hefty blow on the back by the master's big stick. He did not solve the Koan by his reasoned answer. The solution to the Koan is that there is no reasoned answer. To break through the Koan is to break through to the reality beyond intellect, which is the state of being which we have tried to describe as being at center. It is the state of experiencing directly and without purpose. It is the most open, receptive state of being which we know. At center there is that kind of quiet existence which knows calm and soft peace.

And then, aware now of rhythm, we move to the periphery once again where our focus and our acts become purposeful, manipulative, and effectful upon the world around us.

We do not say that center is good and that periphery is bad. We say that to get stuck in either is arrhythmic and therefore not healthy. When we are well we know our rhythm and move with it. Then we are the rhythm, we are center and periphery and the motion from one to the other is like the living breath.

chapter 6

Termination

Psychotherapy is a process of growth. In that sense there is no termination, except in the specific sense that the patient no longer requires psychotherapeutic sessions. He leaves when he can use the tools for his growth by himself. This chapter will be brief, because in effect the entire book has already described how termination is achieved.

THE PATIENT TERMINATES

In most cases the innuendo to terminate comes from the patient. His wish to discuss termination is like a declaration of independence. Whether or not the therapist feels that it is time to terminate is not the point of the matter. The point is that termination has become an issue for the patient. We then discuss it.

It is important to be aware of the patient's purpose. His wish to terminate may represent a resistance to the difficulties he foresees, if he were to take further therapeutic steps. If this is the reason for which he discusses leaving the sessions, then the telltale clue is his sense of dissatisfaction. He is dissatisfied about leaving and he looks toward future events with noticeable pessimism.

This mood is not to be confused with the sadness which may well attend termination. This is, after all, a parting of the way, and readiness to terminate has also a natural note of loss.

In particular circumstances the therapist initiates the topic of termination. This is proper and ethical when the therapist feels he can do no more for the patient who may or may not be ready to terminate. It is quite unethical, we believe, to continue to see a patient when the therapist no longer feels that he can be of help.

Conversely, the patient may wish to terminate but the therapist has clinical reasons to object. It is then mandatory that the therapist be completely confrontive with the patient and explain why in his judgment termination at this time would be a mistake. We suggest this confrontative approach so as to avoid by all means any manipulative or seductive ways of attempting to keep the patient in therapy. But the therapist's "no" must be unmistakable. The point is relevant, because very frequently the patient threatens with termination in order to manipulate the therapist. This threat, in a sense, is his trump card. When the going gets tough for him and he then threatens to terminate, the therapist—so goes the wish—will then let up on him. Confrontation of the topic is then the only way in which manipulation is avoided. In this way a possibly premature termination can be avoided.

INTERMINABLE PSYCHOTHERAPY

The required length of psychotherapy is clearly not a fixed quantity. We have had patients who worked through a phenomenal amount of work in three months and we have had the character problem in which the patient literally accomplished next to nothing after an entire year. Please note in such cases whether the patient might not be coming to reinforce his neurosis. If he establishes the therapist as the authority in his life, then the dependence problem involved is obviously flourishing in a rich soil of support.

There are a significant number of patients who have been in therapy for eight or ten years. We consider it a serious question as to whether their therapy has stunted their growing or has helped them to develop. We have a rule of thumb that helps avoid interminable psychotherapy: If there has been no discernible progress after six months, it is time for a summary of the situation. Furthermore, if we see no significant progress after one year, we would question whether a continued relationship can be useful.

The chronically dependent patient often displays what we call the rubber-ball syndrome. When nothing happens in therapy for a good length of time the therapist might be inclined to put more pressure on the patient. Then the patient responds by showing change. As the therapist eases up, this patient responds by resuming his original symptomatology.

This is a difficult patient to spot and to deal with. Once the rubber-ball syndrome has become clear over a lengthy course of time the prognosis, in our experience, is very guarded.

There is a synonymous situation to the patient who has his neurosis reinforced in psychotherapy. It is the case of the therapist who hangs on to his patient in order to reinforce his own neurosis. Usually, the therapist's dependency needs are similar to his patient's in such situations. He must question his motivation quite seriously when he is keeping a patient in sessions without being sure what is happening in the progress of his patient.

SUCCESSFUL TERMINATION

The simplest sign in this case is the patient who feels good about himself and wants to leave, while the same feeling is reflected in the therapist. Nor is the therapist surprised at the announcement because it has quite organically developed in the recent course of work.

When discussing termination one important topic is the status of change in the patient. The usual signs for completion are improved symptomatology. The presenting complaint has disappeared. And yet this may not always be the case. Uninformed about the nature of therapy, the patient may have commenced work with limited objectives but then turned to the working through of such deep characterological changes that his chief joy of success centers around his new sense of freedom and the new brightness of his world. At the same time, his presenting complaint—such as tension sweats, for example—may not be entirely gone. However, at this point his symptoms are no longer the black banners of his existence but mere annoyances.

Successful terminations may be artificial. The patient moves to another town, the therapist must reduce his workload for personal reasons. Once again we suggest an assessment of the patient's progress at this point of termination. We may suggest further work with another therapist, or we may discuss how the patient can now continue to do remaining work by himself. The parting is open and warm. Incomplete therapy need not mean unsuccessful termination. And the parting, in successful terminations, is always marked by a good, personal relationship. There is acceptance of each other, there is warmth and often friendship.

We consider termination successful even when the patient leaves unaware of remaining, significant characterological problems. We have said that we each grow at our own rate. When the patient's remaining problem becomes an active interference for him, he can return for further work. He may, as it were, have to be processed by life before further change becomes either possible or important.

UNSUCCESSFUL TERMINATION

Clearly, the patient who leaves dissatisfied with his therapeutic work and his progress is terminating unsuccessfully. Although the patient's expectations are not the sole criterion of success, his sense of dissatisfaction indicates unsuccessful therapy. If his realistic goals have not been attained, therapy was lacking. If his unrealistic goals have not been attained, then therapy has not been successful in achieving the patient's realistic orientation.

The patient's unhappiness with results may center on stubborn retention of symptomatology. In that case, therapy has been unsuccessful not because the symptoms are still there, but because the patient has not changed sufficiently in matters of self-support, in characterological flexibility, in order to bear or handle the annoyance of his symptoms.

We must keenly watch for unsuccessful terminations which are largely the therapist's fault. Every therapist has his limitations. No therapist can work with every patient. If we ignore this personal fact for our own neurotic reasons, then the lack of success with a given patient was preordained. If the therapist is saddled with perfectionistic ideals, then he will drive the unfinished patient away because of excessive demands. The first therapist was not in tune with himself, the second one was not in tune with his patient. We wrote this book for both of them.

SAYING GOOD-BYE

When at center, we see what is. When at center, then we see termination for what it is: a parting of the ways. It is that, and no more, and when seen while at center it carries no surcharge of meanings, such as rejection, abandonment, or emotions of loneliness. Good termination means letting go of the old. The attendant emotion is sadness over loss, and joy over walking into the new. This parting by being able to let go of the past, this joy and sadness—that is what we mean by saying good-bye.

Saying good-bye is therefore movement. This movement is possible when those who part do not attempt to possess the other. Such possessiveness in a relationship does not give the possessor another person but only a captive.

The patient who cannot let go of the past relationship is not ready to leave. The one who can cry and laugh when he says good-bye is free.

chapter 7

Outcomes

STANDARDS OF IMPROVEMENT

Most psychotherapeutic methods have clear goals which are derived from the personality theory which have generated the methods. The psychoanalyst, for example, tries to restore the ego to an improved executive function. This is a much more delineated goal than ours, which does not even read too well: expanded experiential awareness.

But our existential approach is not an extrapolation from a tight theory of personality. For that reason we cannot derive a precise pattern of constructs which delineate what the improved patient should be like. As we see it, the goals of psychotherapy can be stated only in very general ways. However, when considering the progress of a particular patient we can describe psychotherapeutic goals in quite individual terms.

Systematic theories of personality contain implicit or explicit definitions of health and pathology. These definitions derive from the set of constructs contained in such theories. They are abstractions about the manner in which people function, and the better a definition the more universal it is. Since a definition applies properly only to a subject which is on the definition's own level of abstraction, then a universal definition of sickness and health applies best to the universal patient. We have never treated one.

But we have found that our individual patients display such varied potentials of feasible growth that their own subjective awareness of acceptable change becomes the pace-setter and the measure of their improvement.

There is another personal basis from which improvement criteria are derived. A therapist will sometimes gauge improvement by the patient's increasing agreement with him.

This situation has been called *congruence.* If the therapist is a much more fully functioning person than the patient and the patient becomes increasingly like the therapist, then this change may be an improvement. It may also be substitution of a minor neurosis for the previous, larger one. But more important, agreement with the therapist is no criterion of improvement since it can be achieved by confluence, with the concomitant loss of the patient's independent identity. Such a relationship between therapist and patient may stabilize in a condition of mutual safety because this "improvement" depends almost entirely upon maintaining the status quo. The condition hardly deserves the name of a therapeutic relationship, although the patient's reduction in pain may well add to the impression that improvement has here taken place.

Degrees of anguish and anxiety are altogether no criteria of the patient's improvement. Any psychological change may be attended by suffering, which means that the improved patient may suffer variously for the rest of his life. But we have distinguished between meaningless and meaningful suffering, where pain may occur due to the stresses of increasing rigidity and the starvation attendant on desensitization, in contrast to the suffering due to the stress of accomplishing a new step in growth.

Quantification attempts have been made in order to give some measure of guarantee that a method of therapy is better than another. We have made no attempt to fix or to render statistics on the number of patients who leave with reduced symptoms or who stay out of therapy for a given length of time. We have not tried to develop these success guarantees because the measures that can be quantitatively stated make no sense in our approach to psychotherapy.

Symptom reduction is no health criterion in the case of the patient whose improved awareness has increased his range of activity and satisfaction because he no longer buckles under the presence of his symptoms.

Duration of therapeutic change is no health criterion in the case of the patient who returns to therapy because a totally new, noxious situation has impinged on his life. Nor does this particular measure of therapeutic worth take into account that the therapeutic requirements or total patient involvement may differ substantially from one series of sessions to another.

But perhaps of most significance is that quantification of success must elude us because the measure of therapeutic success, as we view improvement, depends literally upon the individual patient. And while we have no overall criteria by which we can measure sickness and health, we can describe a number of changes that have been the earmarks of successful psychotherapy.

SUCCESSFUL GROWTH

We will let the patient tell it.

"Therapy? I don't know. It is mysticism but it is pragmatic. It is nothing but it is a fact. It is losing but it is finding. It is a word. Just a word. But it is the most dynamic experience I've ever had. More than this, it has meant the *beginning* of the most dynamic experience—being alive."

Perhaps it is a measure of the very completeness in lived experience that less ability or intent is left over for good verbal description. Therapy causes change; it is change. It is in no case a solution, but it is a gain in the capacity to solve. At termination of therapy we have not seen the patient who ends in euphoria; instead he leaves with a new joy of life. We have seen the calm in one, the eagerness to go out in another. Boundless optimism does not describe the stance of successful growth, but self-trust does—to be again your own friend.

We, and the patient, can describe change through therapy in a number of prevalent areas.

There is an increase in available choice.

"For the first time in my life it seems that I'm not locked into some predetermined series of actions. I'm not in some hideous way forced to pursue a pathway I dislike."

"I simply feel like the complete child—where child means *new*, you know, going out into the world for the first time, like I've never been there before."

"Yes. I do not now feel that I am utterly committed to a bad choice."

This change toward choice reflects a gain in available strength, a willingness, a desire, to experience excitement again.

"I have come away from my hour again and again with a new feeling, a feeling that can best be described as tingling and alive. For a while this was the only experience with another person which I seemed able to have and my whole life revolved around it. It is still a most important event in my life, but at long last I can now look forward to other contacts and—in fact—to living."

"I had expected that therapy would open life to me. But it opened me to life."

This confidence in encounter comes from a knowledge of oneself, an acceptance of oneself. The projections of unacceptable qualities have again been regained as aspects of the self, and there is no blame, no relegating of responsibility, and instead the patient is again an active agent in the shaping of his destiny. He can let go of the past and so live in the present. He no longer disowns himself by projection, he no longer splits himself into ineffectual parts, but instead admits his present self. The neurotic illusion that he can change the past, the preoccupation of regretting lost chances, all this is replaced by an acceptance of the present which is. And that includes himself.

"Well, it's this way. I don't know what I am but I think that there might be something about me that is interesting, something that I could discover. I've been pretty dull most of my life, I've done a lot of interesting things, but I haven't been interested in myself. I have been meaningless. Now I am not. I've got *me*. Which is the baseline from which to start."

To have a full, experiential awareness of oneself means self-acceptance. To be able to see what is—including oneself—means that there is no judgement. The knowledge of *I am* does not require the judgment of *I am good* or *I am bad*. Acceptance involves no judgment at all. As a point of fact, the successful patient is neither self-effacing, self-derogatory, or self-aggrandizing. He is simply what he is.

We are not describing the patient whose self-awareness takes the form of chronic introspection. Posttherapy soul searchers talk about living life at the expense of living it. They psychologize as club members of post-analysands, knowing all the solutions, committing none of the solving. They talk. This is the therapy neurosis.

This newly created neurotic does not yet accept himself. He encounters himself as a problem, not as himself. And as long as he does not accept himself he cannot accept others. When he can, he has achieved the best that therapy can offer. He can love.

Love is a contact with another where giving and receiving are simultaneous events. The loving act is a receptive event. Therefore there is no demand. The loving act is a giving event. Therefore there is no demand. This makes love the state of ultimate satisfaction.

"I have found the way to give without sense of depletion. I am a well. Unused, I grow stagnant. I freshen the well by taking from it, because in that way I renew it."

And this sense of certainty of the self is the best. It means not the end of uncertainty but the strength to do without certainty. This is less than ideal, yet very real. And it is at this point that the patient changes to a self-possessed person again.

"I had thought that my therapist would help me find my real self. Instead, I have found myself real."

We have had successes, but we have no guarantees. Speaking from the center, we have no wish to impose a new system. But, with the same stance, we feel that we can give something new that has worked like a wellspring of aliveness. This is the only condition we know that really describes good therapy, no matter who has devised it.

Then why try what we have to offer? An answer, in this case, is tantamount to a manipulation. We wrote the book because we felt fresh and new about it and because among the many wellsprings of therapeutic aliveness we had not found this one before. And as for the worth of this book, we know that ultimately it is not the system that helps, but the good man who chooses it.